AUDIT CUSTOMER SATISFACTION: MARKETING ADDED VALUE

by

Cindy E. Cosmas

The Institute of Internal Auditors

Disclosure

The IIA publishes this document for informational and educational purposes. This document is intended to provide information, but is not a substitute for legal or accounting advice. The IIA does not provide such advice and makes no warranty as to any legal or accounting results through its publication of this document. When legal or accounting issues arise, professional assistance should be sought and retained.

ISBN 0-89413-373-X
97320 11/96
First Printing

CONTENTS

ABOUT THE AUTHOR

Cindy E. Cosmas has been an auditing professional for more than 12 years. She has an extensive background in banking with several prominent institutions. Her knowledge of manufacturing and defense contracting was obtained through five years of employment at Lockheed Missiles and Space Company. She received degrees in marketing and accounting from Baylor University.

PREFACE SUCCESSFUL MARKETING DOES ADD VALUE

To improve audit customer satisfaction and continuously add value to the organization, a strategic marketing program is an essential auditing tool. Internal auditors must devise specific marketing methods to appeal to management's cost and efficiency expectations. Company-wide issues which should govern the auditor's marketing plan objectives include cost savings, product quality, and customer satisfaction. To add value to the organization's objectives, internal auditing should base their activities on the direction and expectations of organization leaders.

Internal auditors can assess their own knowledge and skills and match them to the organization's needs through development of a comprehensive marketing program. This program should cater to the variable wants, needs, and expectations of their customers. Executive management will support a program which emphasizes an increase in operating profits; operating management will support a program which demonstrates how to increase their productivity.

The purpose of this marketing study is to present a collection of marketing methods which have been successful in furthering the reputation of many internal auditing departments. The marketing techniques contained herein cannot be all things to all people, which is precisely why it is necessary to clarify who will derive the greatest benefit. This study has been structured and geared primarily toward the following audiences:

- Existing internal auditing departments who want to expand their services and increase the quality and quantity of contributions they provide to their organization.
- Contract auditors who are seeking expansion of their services for greater marketability.
- Company management contemplating the feasibility and value of creating an internal auditing department.

This marketing study is applicable to the majority of private and commercial business enterprises as well as government bureaus, their affiliates, and other regulatory agencies. While some people appreciate a theoretical approach to issue development and problem-solving, others relate better to specific guidelines for application, including step-by-step procedures. Both approaches have been incorporated into this study to provide practical methods for applying the suggested marketing techniques.

Preliminary research yielded little related information on the subject of marketing internal audit to achieve audit customer satisfaction; therefore, it was deduced that this concept has, until now, been virtually unexplored. As a result of scarce documented resources, this study primarily relies on the testimony, practical experience, and current marketing techniques and methods used by internal auditors today.

The task of collecting and assimilating the personal experiences of audit professionals from a broad cross-section of industries was inspiring and fruitful. Several prominent individuals were interviewed — individuals who are true entrepreneurs in marketing their internal auditing function. While some of the techniques illustrated in this book are based on traditionally conservative approaches, others incorporate modern variations of marketing approaches, such as state-of-the-art communications technology. It is my sincere hope that the new marketing approaches and techniques presented will prove useful and effective to audit practitioners.

C. E. Cosmas
1996

ACKNOWLEDGMENTS

I offer my sincere thanks to the many members of the auditing profession who supported this effort through their time and energies. The information, company documentation, and other supporting materials they supplied were extremely helpful in making this study come together.

My friends and former colleagues granted me detailed interviews and allowed me a glance at some of their company practices:

- Dean Mayer of Lockheed Martin granted me detailed interviews of his current marketing techniques.
- Kathleen Macina of Charles Schwab provided marketing suggestions and samples of project team packages.
- Michael Messick of Charles Schwab patiently explained some technical, state-of-the-art aspects of his involvement with marketing.
- Elaine Feeny of National Semiconductor contributed her time with interviews regarding her personal experiences with project teams.
- Holly Clark of the Federal Reserve Bank contributed some key marketing facts and data she had collected through her work and from related seminars.
- Elias Nader of Verifone Corporation provided information on how he participated in marketing the startup of his auditing department.
- Janice Thompson of the Federal Reserve Bank shared her professional opinions and personal experience.

To Diane Lutz of Century Bank and Trust in Massachusetts — I owe my appreciation and thanks for her encouragement during this effort. She shared some extremely creative, and truly effective, marketing strategies.

To Jeff Gibbs of Coopers and Lybrand — I owe my heartfelt appreciation for the time he spent giving me pointers and suggestions, helping me organize my thoughts, supplying me with exceptional reference materials, and for his candid and invaluable appraisal of my work.

To Michael Lavine of Sinai Hospital of Baltimore, Inc. — I offer my thanks for his evaluation of several drafts and his helpful suggestions for improving this product.

To Karen Allison of Allison.Com — I owe my appreciation for her creative inspirations and advice on how to best introduce this study.

INTRODUCTION AND CHAPTER OVERVIEWS

> ***The challenge to business management over the next two decades will be coping with change more rapid and deep than ever encountered before. The forces of change sweeping through the economy won't allow much time for contemplation or foot-dragging.***
>
> **— The Kiplinger Washington Letter Editors**
> ***The New American Boom***

Being Flexible to Stay Feasible

Business environments are changing in response to the increased economic pressures currently applied by competition in both domestic and foreign enterprises. Add to this the belt-tightening business consolidations taking place while the number of new markets is decreasing and the majority of mature markets is increasing.[1] Demand for lower prices and higher-quality products is forcing a new way of managing.

As organizations begin trimming their corporate fat, they rid themselves of unnecessary economic barriers and become more financially sound and operationally streamlined. Managerial hierarchies are being flattened and restructured, resulting in fewer managers. As noted by John Zenger of Zenger-Miller, Inc., "Companies everywhere — even blue chips once known for their full-employment policies — are delayering, downsizing, right sizing, early retiring, and/or outplacing their management ranks."[2]

For many managers, trying to downsize an organization's manpower resources while increasing productivity and still maintaining control over the final product can be an organizational nightmare. Managers are discovering that this task cannot be accomplished without some degree of compromising controls or affecting the quality of their product or service. Even

---

[1]Cafferky, Michael E., *Let Your Customers Do the Talking* (Upstart Publishing, 1996), p. 1.
[2]Zenger, John H., Ed Musselwhite, Kathleen Hurson, and Craig Perrin, *Leading Teams: Mastering the New Role* (Illinois/New York: Irwin Professional Publishing, 1994), pp. 3-4.

during downsizing, customers continue to demand improvements in product quality. To meet these demands, managers are forced to question the way their predecessors did business and to reengineer established processes. Managers are rejecting the age-old attitude of "we've always done it that way" and are replacing it with fresh thinking and new, creative ideas for added productivity.

It is during these times of upheaval that internal auditors recognize a tremendous opportunity to become an irreplaceable asset to organization management. Internal auditors have traditionally been placed in the position of having to justify their existence. They can now effectively do just that by demonstrating modern, practical ways of partnering with organization managers in the pursuit of common goals. Successful internal auditors realize that developing an audit strategy consistent with the changing times is inevitable to ensure their future within corporate America. In other words, internal auditing, like every other business venture, is becoming more flexible to stay feasible.

How Auditing Has Evolved

Modern internal auditing has come a long way from dark suits and deceptive audit methods. Traditional auditors boasted numerous, repetitive findings and perpetuated the "us-them" attitude. Today's auditors are doubling their efforts to erase the ill will created in the past and bring about a new approach. This approach is being carefully cultivated in order to inspire real and lasting changes to the old attitudes.

Internal auditors strive to become a commodity sought after by organization managers. Attaining this goal depends largely on the development and implementation of marketing strategies which promote audit skills, capabilities, and services. While marketing a product or service in today's world may seem commonplace and predictable, it is a new concept to try marketing a group of individuals who have traditionally been considered management's adversary.

Effective marketing requires desire, commitment, and an ability to provide quantifiable evidence of cost savings, streamlined operations, and greater economies of scale. Developing a broad marketing plan is the first step; committing to this plan is the second. This concept of marketing their department may be relatively new to most internal auditors. However, those who have already taken the initiative in this direction are reporting positive results, such as an overall improvement in relationships with organization management.

Internal auditors are accepting some diverse challenges in an effort to improve the range and quality of the services they provide to organization management. For example, finding ways to parallel the services offered by business consultants is becoming popular and effective. Business consultants are considered to be the experts in their field, for they offer unique, unbiased perspectives to issues or concerns. Management now views internal auditing as a cost effective alternative to hiring external consultants. As a result of this and other changes in their service philosophy, internal auditors have come full circle from being management's "adversary" to being their "business counselor."

Lawrence B. Sawyer, the celebrated author of many state-of-the-art publications on modern internal auditing, describes auditing practices that are traditionally provided as follows:

- Monitoring activities top management cannot itself monitor.
- Identifying and minimizing operational and financial risks.
- Validating key operating reports.
- Providing information for the decision-making process.
- Reviewing past activities and assessing future ones.
- Assisting line managers in identifying violations of procedures and management principles.[3]

These activities, while still required by many organizations, may seem confining to those internal auditing departments who want to enlarge their scope of work in order to add more value to their organization. Demonstrating ways that internal auditing can benefit the organization in quantifiable terms will enhance their relationship with management and glean more "new business." This study explores new ways that internal auditors can partner with management in the achievement of a common set of goals, thereby improving their working relationships and providing a promising outlook for the future.

---

[3]Sawyer, Lawrence B., and Mortimer A. Dittenhofer, *Sawyer's Internal Auditing: The Practice of Modern Internal Auditing, 4th Edition* (Altamonte Springs, FL: The Institute of Internal Auditors, 1996), pp. 13-14.

Chapter Overviews

The following overviews provide brief summaries of the highlights and key points of each chapter:

Chapter 1 explains how to begin the marketing process. Devising a workable marketing program starts with a well-developed set of objectives which conform with the auditor's charter or mission statement.

Chapter 2 explains how to identify audit customers and define their expectations and needs based on the size of the organization. This chapter also focuses on ways to create an environment of trust between auditors and their customers, how to nurture these relationships, and ways to avoid some common pitfalls. Inherent roadblocks exist to hinder auditors' efforts to establish working relationships with their customers. These roadblocks are built out of preconceived misconceptions of audit techniques, negativism from past audit experiences, or from a fear of involvement with auditors on a human level.

Chapter 3 discusses some practical, yet simple, methods of marketing the internal auditors' image, skills, qualifications, and other important assets. In order to promote their image as management's partner, auditors are using new, and sometimes high-tech, methods of promoting and publicizing themselves and their services. These methods will be described and illustrated with examples when possible.

Chapter 4 explains some proven methodologies for marketing internal auditors as consultants to management. Assisting organization managers in effectively discharging their duties and responsibilities is one of internal auditing's key objectives and challenges. Offering audit services to management results in the development of good working relationships and in internal auditing's image being promoted as a partner, rather than an adversary. In addition, it discusses how the internal auditor can be instrumental in assisting managers assess their current operations and control environments by improving their operational economy and efficiency or automating their operations as appropriate.

Chapter 5 covers an important concept of partnering internal auditing with organization management and personnel through project teams. The team approach has become a fresh, modernistic tool for management in providing independent recommendations to organization problems, in illustrating the scenarios and consequences surrounding impending business decisions, for uncovering information which was previously buried or hidden, and in many other complex business situations. The benefits of implementing teams has been recognized by all. It is because of the unique processes employed by teams and the reliability of their resulting recommendations that organization management has wholeheartedly endorsed their use.

Chapter 6 challenges internal auditing's marketing efforts by finding ways to continuously improve them using a performance measurement system. Measuring performance is considered to be an extremely critical part of the effective management of any activity and can be applied to internal auditing's marketing program. To fully gauge the acceptance and satisfaction of their customers, we will explore some systematic methods of obtaining customer feedback to measure audit effectiveness.

As our business processes and activities advance toward the end of the 20th century, the internal auditing profession is evolving into a service that is flexible and capable of assisting organization managers in a variety of scenarios. Internal auditors have come full circle from their covert role of "police officers" to a modern, cooperative role as "consultants." Organization management is concerned with the economy and efficiency of their operations as well as the effectiveness of their plans to continue identifying opportunities for improvement. In our conclusion, we suggest some activities which may be appropriate for internal auditors willing to continue developing their future marketability.

CHAPTER 1 DEVELOPING MARKETING OBJECTIVES

In the world of modern management, a dual revolution is underway; the manifesto is to manage processes and to mind performance measurements.

— Christopher E. Bogan and Michael J. English
Benchmarking for Best Practices

Accepting the Challenge

Internal auditors who understand the challenges of today's business environment also understand the importance of open communication with organization management. The idea is evolving that internal auditors can play dual roles as auditors and as consultants, which is an extreme departure from their traditional image. This new image is becoming more acceptable to internal auditors who are eager to enlarge and reshape their responsibilities within their organizations.

While internal auditors may be excited about this new role, it has been slow to catch on with many company CEOs. In fact, in a recent study of audit perceptions, only about 30 percent of CEOs polled felt that internal auditors have the skills and expertise to be considered consultants. Gil Courtemanche, author of *Audit Management and Supervision*, states:

> "Internal consulting is a special mode of internal auditing, consisting of the performance of a service specifically requested by management under conditions and guidelines specified by management. Internal consulting may involve finding answers to questions, developing solutions to problems, recommending courses of action, or formulating an opinion."[1]

[1]Courtemanche, Gil, *Audit Management and Supervision* (New York, NY: John Wiley & Sons, 1989), p. 26. Reprinted by permission of John Wiley & Sons, Inc.

Review internal auditors' responsibilities to their organization as directed by their audit charter and The IIA's *Standards for the Professional Practice of Internal Auditing (Standards)* and *Statement of Responsibilities* as follows:

- An auditor's charter or mission statement will generally include comments such as:

  "To assist the audit committee and management....by providing independent review and appraisal....of our internal controls and financial and operational systems....and drive for continuous improvement in the use of company resources."

- *Standard 300* states that "the purpose of the [auditor's] review for quality of performance is to ascertain whether the organization's objectives and goals have been achieved." It goes on to say that internal auditors can offer "assistance to managers who are developing objectives, goals, and systems by determining whether the underlying assumptions are appropriate; whether accurate, current, and relevant information is being used; and whether suitable controls have been incorporated into the operations or programs."

- The *Statement of Responsibilities* clearly states that "the objective of internal auditing is to assist members of the organization in the effective discharge of their responsibilities."

Based on this broadly defined set of responsibilities, internal auditors have a distinct responsibility to support organization management and staff in the achievement of their goals and objectives. In addressing this task, internal auditors must acquire in-depth knowledge of the organization's business and its management team. They cannot continue to perform audits which consist purely of accounting for assets and compliance testing. This traditional approach may not always provide the necessary assistance and value to organization management. Now more than ever, internal auditors' primary goal must be to assist their customers in effectively discharging their duties and responsibilities.

The single best way to accomplish this task may be in performing audits or reviews which are dictated or requested by organization management. Management requests for audit services will increase when internal auditing's marketing program is effectively enacted. There are two basic ways that internal auditors can assist organization management in this manner:

- Internal consulting (Chapter 4).
- Participating on project teams (Chapter 5).

Internal auditors are indeed making a transition to including internal consulting activities as a primary focus. This transition is partly due to an increased pressure for internal auditors to better utilize their accumulated knowledge, thereby increasing the payoff for the organization.[2]

Taking this idea one step further results in the need for a blueprint or strategy for marketing internal auditing's plan for the future. A well-developed marketing plan will provide the basis for selling internal auditing as a company-oriented resource and a partner with management.

What is a Marketing Program?

Professional marketers ask themselves, "What makes buyers buy? What are they looking for?" Marketers know that buyers buy a service as a method of improving pleasure or resolving a problem.[3] As marketers of professional services, internal auditors should ask themselves a similar question: "What will motivate organization management to seek our help?"

One answer evolves from the fact that organization management solicits services from internal auditing primarily to meet their objectives through:

- Resolution of a problem, or;
- Improvement of their operations.

However, there are other reasons they may request consulting services from internal auditing. To:

- Fulfill a need for unique expertise on a short-term project basis.
- Fulfill a need for fresh ideas.

---

[2]Gray, Glen L., and Maryann Jacobi Gray, *Business Management Auditing: Promotion of Consulting Auditing* (Altamonte Springs, FL: The Institute of Internal Auditors Research Foundation, 1994), pp. 1-2.

[3]Katz, Bernard, *How to Market Professional Services* (New York, NY: Nichols Publishing Company, 1988), p. 145.

- Circumvent company politics.
- Fulfill a need for maximum efficiency.
- Train employees.

Another problem stills exists, however, which begs the question, "How can internal auditing demonstrate their professional skills to management and make themselves indispensable?" One answer can be found through the development of an effective marketing strategy.

Any worthwhile endeavor requires foresight and preparation, thorough development of ideas, anticipation of shortfalls, and a backup plan for contingencies. Marketing a professional service like internal auditing requires no less. Relevant activities must be planned and coordinated to be successful. A comprehensive marketing program will be instrumental in identifying customer objectives, matching these objectives to audit services, calculating available audit resources, identifying various channels for communication and promotion, and other details of the plan's strategy.

A marketing program, or plan, is a map to more business. It is a progression of individual steps which includes research, planning, and implementation. This plan should describe a distinct course of action, with the starting point as the goals and objectives of the organization.

A simple, yet effective, marketing plan can be accomplished in five basic steps:

1. *Set marketing objectives.* The key is to set reasonable, manageable objectives in order to avoid becoming overwhelmed. The smaller they are, the easier it will be to accomplish each objective and move on to the next.

2. *Identify the market.* Have a clear understanding of who the customers are and how to satisfy their individual needs.

3. *Choose the promotional tools.* Decide on the best way to reach the customers.

4. *Determine the specific actions to be taken.* Actions should be broken down into small tasks and prioritized. A certain amount of time should be devoted to marketing, which may be best accomplished when properly integrated into a business schedule. Mar-

keting tasks should not require excessive amounts of time or audit resources.

5. *Evaluate the results and improve upon them.* This step is critical because without a way to identify improvements, the marketing plan will stagnate. Understanding how to serve the customer in the most efficient and effective manner is the key to successful continuation.

Developing a feasible marketing plan hinges on many factors, such as information gathering techniques, customer development activities, and marketing research and resources. Meeting the marketing challenge by developing effective methods to market internal auditing's services and capabilities will differ for every organization. Understanding the direction and focus of company leaders will aid in producing results from these marketing efforts.

Identifying Marketing Objectives

To ensure that a comprehensive marketing plan is developed, goals and objectives must be established and understood. Goals are big and relatively abstract, which makes them sometimes difficult to achieve. Objectives are like goals, except they are smaller and more manageable. Marketing objectives, both short-term and long-term, can be the stepping stones toward achieving goals. The following questions should be considered when developing strategic objectives:

- Who are internal auditing's primary and secondary customers?
- What are the goals and objectives of each customer?
- How do these goals relate to the goals of the organization?
- What skills do internal auditors currently possess to satisfy the demands of their customers?
- What services can they provide to assist management in achieving their goals and objectives?
- When, where, and to whom can internal auditing publicize their services?
- What skills will they require to satisfy the future demands of their customers?
- What economic forces or conditions constrain internal auditing's efforts and progress?

- What actions can they take to overcome negative forces?

An effective marketing plan will require preliminary investigation into who the customers are, what services internal auditing can offer them, the amount of time and resources needed to fulfill customer requests, scheduling conflicts, and what benefits both customers and internal auditors will realize from these efforts. The internal auditor's market base will certainly include those who have influence over the organization's operations, those who are routinely audited as part of internal auditing's annual audit plan, or individuals with other connections to internal auditing's activities.

Marketing goals and objectives can be established once the desired results have been identified. Basic goals should be accomplished before pursuing more strategic goals. For example, an internal auditing department may begin with the following basic goals:

- Establish an audit charter with appropriate status and responsibility.
- Acquire the support of organization management and the board of directors.
- Ensure management's support is communicated to organization heads.

Once the basics have been implemented, internal auditing can concentrate on more tactical marketing goals, such as:

- Improve the communication between internal auditing and organizations.
- Build working relationships through performance and professional conduct.
- Promote internal auditing's services as consultants to management.

These goals are still very broad in nature; therefore, some specific objectives should also be considered in conjunction with these goals, as in these examples:

Allocate 20 percent of the audit budget to consulting services (management requests, project teams, etc.); communicate this plan to responsible company managers.

- Meet with all organization heads by midyear to introduce internal auditing's services and to solicit management's concerns.

- Allocate a percentage of each audit to identification of cost savings for all operations (i.e., employ economy and efficiency techniques).
- Attend all upper-level management meetings to keep abreast of pertinent organization issues.
- Present audit progress and accomplishments quarterly to the board of directors.

These objectives are also marketing techniques. Appropriate marketing techniques strive to improve management's perception of the internal auditor's reputation, ability, and integrity. Readers are encouraged to challenge their own objectives by reviewing the questions posed in Exhibit 1.1, which lay the basic groundwork for identifying key audit objectives.

Exhibit 1.1
Questionnaire for Establishing Objectives

1. What are your short-term objectives (within one year)?

2. What are your intermediate objectives (within two to three years)?

3. What are your long-term objectives (within four to 10 years)?

4. List the type of audit projects that your internal auditing staff can currently perform.

5. List the type of audit projects that you anticipate your staff will be performing in one year.

6. Which projects would you consider to be "value-added" to your organization?

On the Path of Progress

The examples of marketing objectives described above are proactive and require dedication and commitment on the part of the entire audit organization. Auditors who insist on employing a *status quo* audit approach will continue to perform mundane, repetitive audits devoid of creativity and thought-provoking interaction with audit customers. Marketing objectives which are employed using well-developed techniques will enable internal auditors to initiate meaningful conversations with management, to delve into the issues that are of consequence to the organization, and to initiate action when appropriate.

When frequently employed, such tools are extremely effective in promoting the consistent interaction with organization management that internal auditors seek and require. As a result of the internal auditors' earnest approach to organization issues, they may find their advice and assistance soon sought after by management.

Now that clear marketing objectives have been established, there are several steps to consider for continuing the marketing plan. The next step, identification of a target market (audit customers), is covered in the next chapter. It sets the stage for:

- Choosing the most effective promotional tools.
- Deciding what specific actions should be taken.
- Monitoring success and developing ways to improve.

Chapter Summary

A marketing program, or plan, is essential for every internal auditing department. A well-devised plan will direct internal auditors in their quest to provide valuable services to their organization. This plan consists of specific objectives, a well-developed customer base, effective promotional tools, a plan of action, and a way to monitor success.

Understanding your own individual goals and objectives is the first step in preparing a marketing plan. Goals are necessary, but specific objectives will allow objective measurement of individual activities. Measurement is necessary in determining areas of strength and weakness and in deciding how to improve the marketing process. When a marketing plan is properly established and implemented, internal auditors should notice an improvement in management's recognition and perception of their services and capabilities.

CHAPTER 2 IDENTIFYING AUDIT CUSTOMERS AND THEIR NEEDS

Successful selling, as every successful salesperson knows, is based on two steadfast requirements: Know your product. Know your customer.

— Lawrence B. Sawyer
The Practice of Modern Internal Auditing

Who are Internal Auditing's Customers?

To sell a product, providers must know their customers intimately. The goal of marketing is to understand the customers so well that the product or service fits them and sells itself. With respect to identifying and developing a customer market base, Peter Block stated in his book, *Stewardship:*

> "Auditing units have the most difficult role in choosing how to serve the institution. They are required by regulation in many cases to perform a policing function in service of top management. At the same time they want to support line managers in performing better. Auditing has a choice, though. They can give emphasis to policing and protection or they can give emphasis to learning and consultation."[1]

The first step, then, in providing meaningful audit services is to determine exactly who will be the recipient of the service, or, the audit customer. Every industry or market has a distinct group of customers, but identifying and serving internal auditing's customers may not be a simple task.

Customer development is a key issue and an activity which must be foremost in planning and cultivating. Each audit customer is important in his

[1]Block, Peter, *Stewardship* (San Francisco, CA: Berrett-Koehler Publishers, 1993), p. 142.

or her own way, and each maintains a set of needs and requirements. The success of internal auditing's marketing program will enable them to further their partnership with organization management. This partnership is the predecessor for their future participation in organization activities and decisions.

Conflict may be created within an internal auditing environment because of the various customers to be served. For example, an operating manager could be considered a customer until a significant detrimental finding is discovered, at which time the internal auditor must recognize an obligation to other customers (namely, executive management and the board audit committee) to report the finding. Performing audits may be fraught with similar conflicts, so it is important to understand the intent of each audit and to whom the final report will be disclosed.

To further understand the question of recognizing internal auditing's customers, some examples of organizations with varying sizes and structures have been outlined and described in terms of management and associated auditing needs. Depending on the complexity and structure of each type of organization and the nature of their business environment, the frequency and formality of audits and their reporting requirements will vary accordingly.

Small Organization: Sole Proprietor

A small organization (perhaps a sole proprietorship with approximately one to five employees) may be somewhat informal in its daily routine and record keeping. Many such businesses have not made use of computerized data tracking systems and simply maintain manual records. An organization of this size may employ one full-time auditor as an alternative to contracting an auditor for periodic reviews.

The internal auditor of a sole proprietorship may find that the customer base consists only of the sole proprietor. The auditor may be charged with ascertaining the reliability and integrity of the financial records, reviewing operational controls for breakdowns, and attesting to the overall health of the business. This review may be the sole proprietor's best preparation for future audits by the Internal Revenue Service.

Therefore, the internal auditor must be diligent in performing the review and should thoroughly discuss and resolve all findings with the proprietor.

The auditor will be able to demonstrate value to the proprietor by identifying meaningful deficiencies and by helping to devise solutions which correct the problems and are economically feasible to implement. A complete, honest review will not only benefit the proprietor, but will continuously justify the internal auditor's services.

Medium-Sized Organization: President (company owner); Investors; Organization Managers

A medium-sized organization (with approximately five to 50 employees) is in a unique situation. The organization most likely has an owner, or president, and may be substantially funded by several investors. Depending on the organization's structure and related industry, the owner may employ several managers. In a manufacturing environment, for example, the organization may have managers for engineering, production, quality control, inventory, and shipping.

The organization may be large enough to warrant hiring an internal auditor or several auditors. It may also be large enough that its continuously changing environment hinders the establishment of suitable controls. Controls which are hurriedly established may be easy to circumvent without detection. In addition, an organization of this size is likely to be in an expansion mode, which may also hinder continuation of controls because of constantly changing employee and process requirements.

An organization like this is in need of oversight by a qualified auditor. The internal auditor's primary customer in this case would be the owner of the organization and any significant investors, as they will have a vested interest in the organization's financial and operational condition. In addition, the auditor must rely on the organization managers to provide the internal auditors with necessary information, so a good working relationship must be maintained with them as well. However, for reporting purposes, the auditor should still maintain loyalty to the organization's owner, who is also authorizing payment of the auditor's services.

Here again, it is in the auditor's best interest to provide quality services to the organization's owner by reviewing both the financial and operational aspects of the business. The auditor will be able to justify continued services by providing sound audit conclusions based on factual evidence.

Large Organizations or Corporations: Board Audit Committee; Stockholders; Chief Executive or Financial Officer; Executive Management; Operating Management; External Auditors; Control Agencies

A large organization or corporation (in excess of 51 employees) has a different set of requirements for internal auditors. Many organizations are required by their stockholders, customers, or external government agencies to maintain a fully staffed internal auditing department. Some maintain such a department mainly to offset annual fees paid to external auditors and to provide assurance to management and stockholders that the organization's financial and operational condition is satisfactory.

In order to formally establish and empower an internal auditing department, their charter or mission statement must be approved by organization management, the board of directors, an audit committee, or a combination of the above. The charter establishes the department's position within the organization, defines the scope of internal auditing activities, and authorizes access to records, personnel, and physical properties relevant to the performance of audits.

Once a formal charter is established, internal auditing has pledged their allegiance and loyalty to executive management, generally the CEO and his or her staff. The relationship between management and the board audit committee will depend on the structure and political needs of the organization. Generally, the audit committee, a subcommittee of the board of directors, has the responsibility of overseeing and approving the internal auditing department's short-term and long-term audit plan. The internal auditor's secondary customer in this case will include operating management, external auditors, and internal control agencies.

A Shifting Customer Base

Modern internal auditors once preferred to view their primary customer as executive or senior management mainly due to the increased influence that these managerial levels wielded within the organization. The market preference of these auditors began shifting and subtle changes evolved, and the market focus now rests squarely on both executive management and the board audit committee.

A new breed of auditors subsequently emerged, termed by Gil Courtemanche as "neo-modern" auditors, who are oriented toward a multiservice, multi-customer approach. This new breed declares that their intention is to provide audit and consulting services to the entire organization — from the audit committee down to all levels of operating management and external organizations.

As a result of this change, a new approach to internal auditing has been embraced, which results in a broadening of the market base requiring audit services. Thus, the customer markets of most large, established organizations to be served currently include:

- The board audit committee.
- Executive management.
- Operating management.
- External auditors.
- Control agencies.

Each should be served in a manner appropriate with their authority, responsibilities, and business needs.[2]

Board Audit Committee

Until recently, the board audit committee maintained a corporate "monopoly" as internal auditing's sole customer. While internal auditing's entire customer market was comprised of the audit committee, their mutual suspicion and mistrust belied what appeared to be an intimate relationship.

This relationship has improved since then, but even today, many members of board audit committees are outside organization directors who possess little knowledge of, and have little financial stake in, the organization. Nevertheless, internal auditors must respect that when audit committee members are nominated to a position of authority, they are given specific responsibilities for overseeing portions of the organization's affairs.

Internal auditors are generally unaware of an audit committee's purpose and charter responsibilities, which mainly include corporate governance, financial reporting, and internal accounting control based on the require-

[2]Courtemanche, Gil, *Audit Management and Supervision* (New York, NY: John Wiley & Sons, 1989), pp. 53-57.

ments stipulated by the public accounting profession and the Foreign Corrupt Practices Act. Internal auditing has an obligation to meet the expectations of the audit committee, which include:

- Ensuring that the internal auditing staff consists of educated, professional individuals of quality.
- Ensuring that the objectives and scope of the audit program are developed in accordance with basic organization criteria.
- Providing assurance that organization business is conducted in compliance with legal and ethical standards.
- Providing guidance for protecting the organization's reputation.
- Protecting the dignity, integrity, and reputation of organization management.
- Providing guidance and information to avoid potential issues resulting from unwanted legal liability.

While the internal auditing function assumes several responsibilities to their audit committee, the audit committee can also wield significant political leverage on internal auditing's behalf. To sustain the momentum in their continuously developing relationship and to successfully serve the needs of their organization, both entities rely on mutual support and personal integrity.[3]

Executive Management

Based on the evolution of internal auditing's market development, we can safely affirm that executive management is considered to be one of internal auditing's primary customers. In order to fulfill executive management's needs, internal auditors should first understand what those needs are and how they relate to the welfare of the organization. Practical experience and management testimony indicate the following:

- ***Monitoring operations***. Executive management is responsible for monitoring corporate operations, identifying problems, and resolving the problems with the help of operating management. While executive management will concede that problems can and do exist in most operations, they can become indignant when internal auditors lack the proper perspective in identifying and re-

[3]Ibid, pp. 67-77.

solving issues which are deemed materially insignificant. In these instances, executive management considers internal auditing itself to be a problem through their insidious wasting of an operating manager's time and energy. Executive management appreciates internal auditors who are able to work with responsible operating management to resolve problems that are appropriate for this level, rather than unnecessarily elevating issues to executive management.

- ***Performing special assignments***. Fulfilling the needs of executive management can present special challenges for internal auditors. They must resist the temptation to focus solely on the technical aspects of the assignment. They should be alert for situations which may involve improper political involvement. While encouraging special assignments from executive management, internal auditors should avoid situations where their independence may be compromised and their relationship with executive management could potentially suffer.

- ***Serving the audit committee***. One of internal auditing's tasks in serving executive management is to adequately support the audit committee. Internal auditing must be sensitive in communicating to executive management their audit findings before needlessly alarming the audit committee and possibly causing an embarrassing situation for executive management.

- ***Conforming to leadership patterns of the organization***. The chief executive's primary concern is leadership. Leadership patterns dictated by the CEO and other members of executive management must be observed by internal auditors in performing their audits. Audit findings must be reported in a manner consistent with those leadership patterns. Accordingly, audit reports should avoid disclosures which may only serve to restrict future audit activities.

- ***Loyalty to senior management***. Internal auditing must remain loyal to the CEO. This loyalty conforms with the board's desire that internal auditing work closely with the CEO and support his or her business decisions and organization policies. The board expects internal auditing to defer to the CEO's judgments and accept his or her instructions for monitoring organization operations.[4]

[4]Ibid, pp. 93-106.

Operating Management

The audit climate is changing with the emergence of modern marketing techniques which strive to draw operating management into its circle of customers. Operating managers have distinct, specific needs that can be fulfilled by internal auditors. This statement is a clear departure from traditional auditing where internal auditing's customer was exclusively considered to be the board audit committee.

Operating managers may need help in researching a potential or known problem for which they have neither the labor resources nor the expertise. In some cases, managers may not have the necessary support from upper management to resolve an identified problem. Enlisting the auditors' aid may result in the attention the managers have been looking for in resolving their issues. Internal auditors have a responsibility toward operating management in providing whatever assistance is reasonably possible in meeting their operational goals and objectives.

Internal auditors have been looking for ways to reconcile their traditional reputation with operating management. Internal auditors may find additional ways to justify their existence by assisting managers in resolving their internal issues. Auditors have the independence necessary to review a questionable situation, determine the seriousness and consequences of the pertinent issues, develop feasible alternatives, report their recommendations to relevant personnel, and monitor resolution of the issue. This concept, known as partnering with management, is discussed in detail in Chapter 4.

External Auditors

Internal auditors recognize external auditors as important customers. Consistent communication between external and internal auditors can result in a mutually beneficial relationship. As stated in Section 550 of the *Standards for the Professional Practice of Internal Auditing (Standards)*, the director of internal auditing has the responsibility of coordinating internal and external auditing efforts "to ensure adequate audit coverage and to minimize duplicate efforts." Coordination of audit efforts includes, at a minimum:

- Periodic meetings to discuss matters of mutual interest.
- Access to each other's audit programs and working papers.
- Exchange of audit reports and management letters.

- Common understanding of audit techniques, methods, and terminology.[5]

Periodic meetings and open, honest sharing of audit ideas and workpapers are beneficial to both internal and external auditors. External auditors who feel confident about the internal auditors' skills, knowledge, and audit techniques will likely rely on the internal auditors' workpapers. The external auditor may rely heavily on the internal auditors' work to the extent that the internal auditing department improves internal accounting control throughout the organization. This reliance will reduce the external auditors' risk, effort, and scope of review, which translates into decreased work hours and fees charged to the organization. Therefore, internal auditors may be able to quantify their services to management by helping to reduce the cost of external auditors.

However, the external auditor must still make an independent judgment as to the organization's system of internal control. The function of the external auditor is to provide assurance that the organization's financial statements fairly represent the results of operations in accordance with generally accepted accounting principles. When relying on the internal auditor's work, the external auditor must be satisfied with the competence and objectivity of the internal auditor. The external auditor may want to evaluate the qualifications of individual auditors, the hiring, firing, and training practices of the internal auditing department, and the scope and findings of the audits performed.

A concern exists regarding the increased liability of external auditors, which has caused internal auditors to expand their reviews correspondingly. With the passage of the Foreign Corrupt Practices Act (FCPA) in 1977, organizations became more aware of the requirement of maintaining good systems of control. The result of this act was to provide a significant boost to internal auditing.

The FCPA requires all public companies to establish and maintain reasonably complete and accurate accounting records and devise a sufficient system of internal accounting controls. These controls should provide reasonable assurance that transactions are properly authorized and recorded, assets are protected and periodically verified, and that all accounting transac-

---

[5]Gleim, Irvin N., *CIA Review: Sixth Edition* (Gainesville, FL: Gleim Publications, Inc. 1994), p. 120-122.

tions are treated in accordance with generally accepted accounting principles. The purpose of these requirements is to prevent bribes to foreign and domestic officials and businesses from being buried in other accounts. Internal auditors are now considered major players in the effort to ensure the adequacy of control systems.

The internal auditor is concerned with any outside services rendered to ensure that the organization receives the most benefit for its expense. Internal auditors can also benefit from utilizing workpapers prepared by external auditors. Reliance on the external auditors' workpapers will reduce duplication of effort, which will please organization management, since they are obligated to allow their employees to spend time working with the auditors during an audit. Less time required of operating management and their employees results in a more productive environment and cost savings.

The relationship with external auditors should be a continuing partnership involving coordination of audit efforts. Coordination between these associates can be achieved in several ways:

- Internal auditors can provide external auditors with copies of the long-range internal auditing program.
- Internal auditors can provide external auditors with copies of all internal audit reports which document audit coverage, adequacy of control, and corrective action on deficiencies.
- Internal auditors can schedule reviews of certain operations and related accounts to coincide with the external auditor's needs.
- Both auditors can exchange workpapers when appropriate.
- Internal auditors can assist external auditors by performing compliance and substantive tests.

Control Agencies

Internal auditing may not be the only group to monitor the control aspects of their organization. Most large organizations maintain a number of control agencies which specialize in monitoring specific, technical organizations. These agencies may have an equal or greater interest in the organization's control environment and should be included in plans for reviews. For example, consider the following internal control agencies:

- ***Security departments*** are concerned with controls over sensitive organization data or products, protection of organization interests, and security of organization facilities.

- ***Quality control departments*** are concerned with controls which ensure necessary inspections and certifications are performed to support product reliability and quality.
- ***Safety departments*** are concerned with controls over facility and fleet maintenance, accident prevention, and corrective actions for reported incidents.
- ***Resident government audit groups*** are concerned with ensuring that documentation contains proper authorizations, that errors are properly identified and corrected, and that policies and procedures are kept current.

Coordination with control agencies will result in a valuable exchange of ideas. When proper communication between internal auditing and these agencies is established, duplication of effort will be reduced. In addition, areas which warrant special audit emphasis may be identified. Internal auditors may be able to utilize the expertise from individuals within these organizations to properly classify deficiencies and devise corrective actions. There are several ways to coordinate with internal agencies:

- Meet periodically to exchange audit schedules and ideas. Understand what areas are of concern to each organization and how controls may be circumvented to allow improprieties or fraud to occur.
- Offer to assist in investigations which indicate potential control breakdowns. Many times, internal auditors are able to obtain records and other pertinent data more readily and efficiently.
- Distribute audit reports to relevant agencies for their information and/or feedback. Request that they also communicate the results of their investigations to internal audit.[6]

Participation versus Confrontation

Of all the challenges facing internal auditors, interfacing with their customers while effectively performing their audit duties may be the most challenging. Inherent in this relationship is the perception that auditors are bent on reporting every error discovered, no matter how insignificant, in an attempt to justify their existence and earn credit with management.

[6]Sawyer, Lawrence B., and Mortimer A. Dittenhofer, *Sawyer's Internal Auditing: The Practice of Modern Internal Auditing,* 4th Edition (Altamonte Springs, FL: The Institute of Internal Auditors, 1996), pp. 1009-1010.

In actuality, audit customers may know very little about an auditor's role and purpose, depending on the customer's level of experience with audits. Internal auditors must understand that, in order to conduct an audit in the most effective manner possible, a new perception of their role and purpose must be created and nurtured.

Recently, what we would consider to be traditional or hard-line auditing techniques are being replaced with consultative methods. Traditional auditors relied on a surprise factor to gain an edge over the auditee. Communication was strained at best, and auditors willingly accepted their "police officer" image. Other conditions which distinguished traditional internal auditors include the following:

- Auditors often displayed superior, smug, or condescending attitudes toward auditees.
- A distinct separation of roles was maintained.
- Reports contained detailed account of deficiencies and auditor recommendations.
- Reports seldom mentioned positive conditions.
- Judgments were inflexible and few errors were tolerated.
- Standards for operation were imposed by the auditor.
- Confrontational attitudes between the auditor and the auditee were common.

Sawyer explains that:

> "Many auditors contribute to [negative] perceptions through their failure to understand why auditees act as they do in the presence of an auditor. Nearly all conscious behavior is motivated or caused. Internal auditors who have no understanding of motivational theory will cause behavior which place roadblocks in front of their audit objectives. People receive motivation from their underlying needs and act in a way to satisfy those needs. They react negatively and hostilely when those needs are threatened."[7]

Internal auditors are bound by their code of ethics to exercise honesty, objectivity, and diligence while performing their duties and responsibilities.

[7]Ibid, p. 1230.

They should not knowingly participate or be implicated in any activities relating to fraud, wrongdoing, or any other illegality. They are still obligated to report, to the best of their knowledge, all material facts which may have an impact on the operations under review. Therefore, even though an auditor strives to maintain a positive relationship with the management and staff being audited, he or she is still responsible for disclosing deficiencies and recommending appropriate corrective actions.

The following suggestions for performance are intended to boost the auditor's awareness of his responsibility to his customers and to motivate him to adopt a participatory approach during reviews:

- Understand the customer's needs and expectations.
- Satisfy these requirements.
- Be prompt, courteous, and professional.
- Communicate properly with customers.
- Address and resolve difficult situations.
- Overcome resistance and other negative attitudes.[8]

Actions Speak Louder Than Words

Good communication skills help to form good relationships with auditees. In addition, auditors will find that when open two-way communication with the audit customer is maintained, the audit will be conducted with greater efficiency. It is more likely that the audit customer will be more receptive to correcting deficiencies and ensuring compliance with suggestions.

Irvin N. Gleim, well-known author of CPA and CIA self-study handbooks, states that "recent research has disclosed substantial benefits resulting from establishment of a cooperative (participative) audit approach. This approach is based on behavioral science research into the theory of motivation. The following findings tend to support this approach:

- People are motivated to contribute to any activity in direct relationship to the personal benefits or rewards they might obtain from that activity.
- People are more likely to accept changes if they have participated in the decisions and in the methods used to implement changes.

[8]Hutchins, Greg, *ISO 9000 Implementation Manual* (Vermont: Oliver Wight Publications, Inc., 1994), p. 95.

- Feelings of mutual liking and trust contribute to amicable relationships, which produce a more favorable environment for the audit effort."[9]

Modern internal auditors must learn how to balance their independence and audit judgment with a more empathic, understanding attitude toward their auditees. Instead of conducting the audit in a negative manner, auditors should seek out the candid concerns of auditee management in an effort to portray a participative style of auditing. As a result of this behavioral change, internal auditors are noticing that their interpersonal relationships with audit customers are steadily improving. Other changes which are characteristic of a participative audit approach include the following:

- Auditor and audit customer jointly agree upon the benchmark for operational standards.
- Reports are balanced to include audit customer commendations and credit when appropriate.
- Internal auditor's role is transitioning into more of a consultant.
- Procedures are questioned for viability, relevance, and good sense.
- Internal auditors consult with management in an effort to improve efficiency and productivity.

Auditors need the help of their audit customers during a review. The audit customer is the expert and can provide a clear understanding of the operations or functions being reviewed. Technical personnel within the organization may be able to interpret audit tests and help the auditor understand test results and their implications. When deficiencies are found, these personnel can frequently assist in devising a plan to correct the unsatisfactory condition disclosed by the audit.

Studies have shown that auditing with a consultative, participatory style results in not only good audit customer relations, but a greater possibility that audit findings will be corrected in a timely manner. Participation can demonstrate to operating management that internal auditors are interested in improving the operating process, not in accumulating audit findings.

This style of auditing will enable all parties involved to reap the benefits. Internal auditors will enjoy a relaxed atmosphere with their audit custom-

[9]Gleim, Irvin N., *CIA Review: Sixth Edition* (Gainesville, FL: Gleim Publications, Inc. 1994), p. 419.

ers and may be able to glean more candid and informative answers to their questions. Likewise, audit customers may be able to gain support from the auditors on issues for which their management previously showed little interest. The implication is that audit style and approach are equally as important as technical competence. Clearly, actions can speak louder than words.

Conflict and Fear

Inevitably, conflicts will arise during an audit. Some directly relate to the auditor's objectives and are inherently present. On one hand, an auditor strives to develop and maintain a positive relationship with the audit customer. It is important to secure cooperation and confidence from the operating manager under review. Most importantly, the auditor wants to ensure that the manager will implement corrective action on audit findings. On the other hand, the auditor must be alert to identifying fraud or any other wrongdoing, and must maintain independence and identify and report deficiency findings, even if the report cites findings which may be detrimental to the manager.

There can be an element of fear for the audit customer before, during, and after an audit. This fear may exist because the audit customers believe that an audit will result in criticism or punishment due to adverse findings, loss of personal goals, deprivation of need satisfaction, changes in daily tasks or processes, or punitive action taken by superiors.

When an audit customer displays such fear or mistrust, the auditor can expect less cooperation, a more formal attitude from the audit customer, guarded answers to questions, and information which is brief, incomplete, or unreliable. In addition, audit customers may tend to withhold relevant information from the auditor when they perceive the auditor unfavorably.

The fear of criticism may at times provoke strong emotional reactions from audit customers. An audit customer may react with an attitude of defensiveness, resentment, and hostility toward the auditor. The audit customer may recognize the value in an independent appraisal of his work; however, accepting the disclosure of errors can be difficult. Unfortunately, negative feelings generated toward one auditor may be transferred to other auditors. In addition, auditors may have to convince their customers that they understand the process they are auditing and are competent to make recommendations.

The fear felt by some audit customers may not be wholly unfounded. Those who have experienced past audits may be reacting to other auditors and their methods. Insensitive audit practices of the past may have alienated audit customers and, unfortunately, propagated their attitude. The following are elements of an unfavorable, negative auditing methodology:

- Reports that are overly critical, focusing only on deficiencies.
- Mysterious audit objectives and techniques that make audit customers uneasy.
- Seeking to attach blame for errors.
- The perception that auditors personally gain from reporting deficiencies.
- Hostile, smug, antagonistic, or superior audit styles.
- Conducting conversations in a stiff, formal manner.
- Lack of understanding or empathy for the audit customer's problems.
- Focusing on insignificant errors.
- More time spent scrutinizing defects instead of trying to improve operations.
- A prosecutorial, inflammatory style of questioning.

Dispelling Auditee Fears

Many fears can be dissuaded with the proper approach by the internal auditor. When an atmosphere of trust and honesty is present, the audit customer is more likely to be cooperative and to participate in the audit. The following techniques may be useful in creating an atmosphere of trust and in building a positive auditor/audit customer relationship:

- ***Explain internal auditing's charter and reporting responsibility***. The audit customers should understand that an internal auditor's charter gives him access to all necessary documents and individuals during the course of the audit. In addition, per the *Standards*, the auditor's primary responsibility is to be "an independent appraisal function within an organization to examine and evaluate its activities as a service to the organization." Therefore, the auditor has a responsibility to organization management to report any significant deficiencies which may be of consequence to the operations.

- ***Tell the audit customer exactly how findings will be reported.*** It is helpful if both the auditor and audit customer initially agree on what would constitute a significant deficiency worthy of inclusion in a report. Significant issues will require the audit customer to propose a plan of corrective action. Audit customers should be aware that, if implementation has occurred prior to report issuance, their prompt response in correcting the deficiency will also be noted in the report.

The auditor should also discuss how minor deviations or isolated human errors will be handled; generally these deficiencies should only be reported if other mitigating circumstances influence the auditor's judgment. Corrective action for all findings should be developed by company management with concurrence from the auditors. The auditors should be prepared to offer evidence to their customers supporting their findings.

- ***Set a professional tone***. Professional behavior by the auditor is key to setting the tone of the audit. A competent attitude and complete disclosure of what can be expected during the course of the audit will enable the auditor to gain the trust and confidence of the audit customer.

- ***Establish a line of communication***. Discussions with company management and personnel should be candid, open, and honest. The method of communicating interim audit results should be determined and agreed upon at the beginning of the audit. The audit customer should feel comfortable that the auditor will periodically provide updates on the status of the audit and report issues as they arise. Only in situations where fraud is suspected or when verifying assets on hand should the method of communication be modified appropriately.

Fears mainly arise from the unknown. If organizations know exactly what they can expect, then audit results should not come as a surprise. Audit fairness stems from avoiding unnecessary surprises. On the other hand, an auditor cannot look the other way when deficiencies are obvious. Organization managers have a right to fair treatment, but they have no right to hide deficiencies from the auditors.

Section 280.03 of the *Standards* maintains that "when an internal auditor suspects wrongdoing, the appropriate authorities within the organization should be informed." The internal auditor can be considered an extension of executive management. Therefore, he has an obligation to uphold the responsibilities which have been bestowed upon him by company management. As Sawyer so convincingly argues:

> "Many senior executives see the internal auditor's role as more than a detector of wrongdoing. They want their internal auditors to be a part of the problem-solving team, working shoulder-to-shoulder with operating management to correct weaknesses deficiencies. But senior managers also want to be assured of the internal auditor's protective role. Internal auditors must make sure that systems are properly controlled and protected. The *Standards* require internal auditors to be alert to the possibility of intentional wrongdoing, errors, omissions, inefficiency, waste, ineffectiveness, and conflicts of interest. Further, when internal auditors suspect wrongdoing, they should inform appropriate authorities within the organization. The internal auditor does have a watchdog function and must be aware of the ever-present danger of management fraud."[10]

In light of this, internal auditors must be prepared to deal with audit customers on two different levels: they must deal fairly and openly with their customers, yet they must disclose wrongdoing uncovered during an audit. Internal auditors are bound by their charter, by their *Statement of Responsibilities*, and by the *Standards* to uncover hidden defects and report them to the proper authorities. Still, this can generally be accomplished while employing a humanistic behavior toward audit customers. While fair dealing must not be considered synonymous with whitewashing, internal auditors who adopt a participative posture with their audit customers usually stand a better chance of attaining their audit objectives than those who do not.[11]

---

[10]Sawyer, Lawrence B., and Mortimer A. Dittenhofer, *Sawyer's Internal Auditing: The Practice of Modern Internal Auditing,* 4th Edition (Altamonte Springs, FL: The Institute of Internal Auditors, 1996), pp. 1260.

[11]Ibid, p. 1263.

Chapter Summary

Identifying audit customers is only the first step in developing services that will be desirable and valuable. Internal auditors must understand the motivations and objectives of their customers in order to provide services which will meet their wants, needs, and desires. This understanding will enable the internal auditor to also develop long-lasting relationships and form a basis for future activities and projects.

The philosophy of auditor/audit customer relationships has shifted. Modern auditors are rejecting the attitudes of their predecessors which kept auditees at arm's length and encouraged an air of mystery. Auditors are building trust and establishing open lines of communication in an effort to promote confidence and form long-term relationships with their auditees.

Investing the time and effort in developing lasting relationships will benefit both internal auditors and their customers. Only through mutual respect and understanding can this be accomplished. Internal auditors must be able to dispel audit customer fears through ongoing communication, professional behavior, rejection of petty or diminutive audit techniques, and a non-confrontational manner. Auditors must also learn how to balance their audit duties and responsibilities with a firm, yet responsive, attitude in order to properly serve the needs of their customers.

CHAPTER 3
MARKETING AUDIT SERVICES

It is not the work we do that makes us professionals; it is the spirit in which we do it.

— Lawrence B. Sawyer
Sawyer's Internal Auditing: The Practice of Modern Internal Auditing

What is Marketing?

A business is uniquely set apart from all other human organizations by the fact that it *markets* a product or service.[1] *Marketing* can be defined as those functions involved in transferring goods or services from producer to consumer, including buying, selling, storing, transporting, standardizing, risk bearing, and supplying market information. Marketing is accomplished by identifying the needs of customers and satisfying those needs by selling the appropriate service or product.[2]

The average consumer would probably define marketing as a combination of advertising, promoting, and selling. In fact, however, marketing also includes product planning, new product development, developing customer attitudes through public relations, and distributing products and services.

Successful marketers are constantly in touch with their customers' needs and wants. As a result, they are able to deftly anticipate and plan which products will be willingly accepted. Therefore, services and products are provided as a result of demand. Demand is highly volatile and constantly changing. Marketing a service may be especially challenging because of the way customers change their perception of needs as the market also changes.

---

[1]Drucker, P. F., *Management: Tasks, Responsibilities, Practices* (New York, NY: Harper & Row, 1974), p. 62.

[2]Katz, Bernard, *How to Market Professional Services* (New York, NY: Nichols Publishing Company, 1988), p. 5.

A marketing program should not be strictly consumed by the question, "What do we want to sell?," but more importantly, "What does the customer need?" The marketing revolution has undergone significant changes in philosophy since the early 1900s, when the typical goal of the American businessman was to sell what he had produced. Today, the goal is to produce what is needed. Therefore, instead of saying "This is what we do," the service provider now understands that "These are the satisfactions the customer looks for, values, and needs."

Promotional Tools

In order for internal auditors to truly market their services, they must be able to identify their customers, search out their needs by identifying their objectives, and, finally, market their services by publicizing their expertise. Marketing audit services is a tricky business. There is the question of providing a service while faithfully adhering to the audit charter. In addition, independence must still be maintained at all costs. However, the gap between auditing an operation and assisting a customer can be bridged to some degree while preserving an unbiased opinion and independence.

To effectively market internal auditing's expertise, the needs of their customers must be defined and audit services must be tailored to meet those needs. Effective marketing of internal auditing's services should start with the audit manager. The audit manager has significant exposure to and influence over the members of executive management and the board audit committee. The audit manager is in a good position to candidly solicit concerns from organization managers. He or she is responsible for ensuring that audit customers are aware of the qualifications of his or her staff and how their services could benefit each organization.

Promotional activities for audit professionals are described as those activities designed to promote the image and progress of those individuals. Customer acceptance of audit services stems from their awareness of what those services are and how they can be utilized. The promotional objectives of the audit manager include:

- Building awareness of audit services among current and potential customers.
- Communicating the benefits derived from audit services.
- Building a favorable image.

- Persuading customers to request the auditor's services.
- Eliminating preconceived misconceptions.[3]

In order to market internal auditing's services, the audit manager must first capture management's attention, then earn their confidence. This is accomplished through consistent and effective advertising and promotion.

The *merchandising theory* may be effectively applied to the internal auditor's marketing strategy. According to this theory, merchandising must be the central part of any marketing program. The market must be properly segmented in order to identify potential customers, and the approach must accommodate the fact that each customer has a number of sometimes conflicting wants and needs that must be satisfied. These wants and needs are influenced by background or conditioning, the immediate situation confronting the customer, and, most importantly, what he or she knows about the audit services either directly or vicariously through communication with others.

The desire for audit services is influenced by its accessibility and the effort required to secure it. Yet the potential exists that audit services may be presented in such a way that they satisfy the most important of the customer's wants, needs, and desires. This requires presentations to the audit customer; feedback from the customer; analysis of the customer's wants, needs, and desires; and calculation of the best way to satisfy them.[4] Presenting audit services to their customers should begin with the following marketing methods:

Set aside audit resources for management-requested reviews. A designated percentage of audit resources should be set aside in the annual audit plan for the sole purpose of serving customers through management-requested reviews of operations. There are several effective methods by which to inform organization management of the availability of these resources:

1. ***Presentations to the audit committee.*** An excellent method of marketing available audit resources is for the audit manager to present the audit plan at meetings with executive-level managers. In the presentation, the audit manager could discuss the audit resources in terms of man-hours that have been set aside in anticipation of consultative re-

---

[3]Ibid, p. 66.

[4]Cohen, William A., *How to Make It Big As a Consultant* (New York, NY: American Management Association, 1991), pp. 61.

views, internal auditing's primary service to organization managers. These meetings are also the perfect vehicle for the audit manager to introduce other audit services (i.e., participation on project teams) and the technical skills of the auditors.

2. ***Presentations to organizations***. Another method of communicating the availability of audit resources is to meet informally with organization management and their staff and present a synopsis of audit services. These presentations may be informally planned either during the performance of an audit or at another prearranged time. These meetings will provide auditees with an opportunity to ask questions about the audit process, reporting process, and other issues of concern.

3. ***Encouraging audit customer participation***. An effective, but little used, method of marketing audit's resources is to involve organization management in the preparation of the annual audit plan. This approach requires a comprehensive review of organization issues and concerns through interviews with cognizant organization managers. Based on the managers' input and concerns, a thorough risk analysis can be prepared to indicate which areas pose the greatest risk to the organization and should be scheduled early in the audit cycle. In addition, ideas for management requests may be generated and scheduled. By requesting management's participation in this process, audit customers will gain a feeling of empowerment over the audit schedule, and their resistance during the actual audit will diminish.

4. ***Direct written communication***. The audit manager may consider a mass mailing to all organization heads to publicize the available audit budget for use at their discretion. This method is direct and invites an immediate response by organization managers.

Be alert to relevant organization and industry issues. The audit manager is responsible for staying abreast of organization or industry-wide issues which impact specific organizations. Once a concern becomes apparent, the audit manager should immediately communicate the issue to responsible organization management. When the responsible manager is contacted, the audit manager should offer audit assistance in the form of a consultative review. By being well-informed on subjects which may affect organization interests, management will begin to rely on the audit manager for continued input, opinion, and advice on related matters. An example of one audit director taking action to market her department in response to an impending federal regulation is illustrated in Exhibit 3.1.

Exhibit 3.1
Complying With Federal Regulations

Banks must comply with the Federal Deposit and Insurance Corporation Improvement Act (FDICIA) once they acquire $500 million in assets. The audit director of a small bank carefully monitored her bank's asset base, which exceeded $500 million at the end of 1995. In 1996, she informed bank management of the requirement for the bank to now adhere to the regulation and began a campaign to promote compliance.

She initiated her campaign by setting aside 500 hours of her 1996 audit budget in anticipation of her staff assisting the various organizations in achieving the necessary compliance. Next, she met with executive management and key organization managers to inform them of her plan to audit each department's compliance. With the help of the managers, the audit director established dates of completion for each organization. This regulation requires each department manager to:

- Provide a complete risk analysis of their department.
- Indicate mitigating controls for each risk identified.
- Identify where the controls are documented.
- Indicate the personnel who are responsible for ensuring compliance.
- Update their policies and procedures to include the controls.

Because this project was spearheaded by the audit director, company management began to consider this task to be an unnecessary exercise in drudgery. As a result, some managers began dragging their feet in meeting compliance with the regulation. The audit director realized that some incentives were needed to give managers a boost to complete the project. She wrote and distributed the following letter:

Exhibit 3.1 (Cont.)

TO: FDICIA Implementation Team
FROM: Team Captain (Audit Director)
SUBJECT: Season Warm-Up

The team is off to a good start with most players actively participating. There have been a couple of benchwarmers, but with the proper training and motivation, I'm sure we can get them in the game. Most players have already met with the Team Captain and are on their way to completing their portions of the game plan. I believe we are heading for a very successful season.

The starting nine have a due date of May 6th. The first of these nine departments to accurately complete their FDICIA Worksheet will be awarded a pizza party for their department! (The second lineup will have an opportunity to win a pizza party on their May 13th due date.) GO TEAM!!!

Distribution:	UMPIRES:	CEO
		President
	COACHES:	Senior Executive Vice President
		CFO and Treasurer
		Other Senior Vice Presidents
	PLAYERS:	Department Managers/Supervisors

The response to this letter was tremendous. *All* of the managers who had not already complied called the audit director the same day they received this letter. As a result of her effective morale building, compliance with the FDICIA regulations was achieved ahead of schedule. This is an excellent example of how positive motivation through creative marketing can work to the auditor's advantage.

There are many sources of information available to internal auditors to enable them to stay abreast of relevant organization and industry issues. The following chart shows some common sources of information for effective scanning of pertinent issues within the business environment.

Inside Sources:	**Outside Sources:**
Annual report	General business publications
In-house public relations	Trade and industry publications
In-house newsletters	Professional organizations
Employee orientation	Conferences
Design reviews	Public workshops and seminars
Training sessions	Customer/supplier forums
Staff meetings (all levels)	Customer/supplier task forces
Quality reports, updates	
Customer feedback surveys	
Budget meetings	
Bulletin boards	
Executive roundtables	
Office services	
People on special task forces	

Use word-of-mouth advertising. Probably the most effective method of marketing internal auditing's services is by word of mouth. Michael E. Cafferky, author of *Let Your Customers Do the Talking*, contends that word of mouth as a method of communication serves the broadest range of operations. It covers the largest proportion of the population when compared with any other single method of advertising. Marketing internal auditing by word of mouth can be extremely useful for several reasons:

- Internal auditing's services are highly intangible, and references from other managers will help promote the positive aspects of their services.
- Internal auditing has a traditionally negative image among company personnel, and continued negativity may harm future relationships.
- Internal auditing has a strong human element to consider, and their customers' opinions will have a significant impact on how internal auditors are perceived.
- There is constant contact between internal auditors and company personnel, which can be an excellent opportunity to influence positive word of mouth.[5]

---

[5]Cafferky, Michael E., *Let Your Customers Do the Talking* (Upstart Publishing, 1996), pp. 204-216.

Word-of-mouth advertising occurs constantly — during audits, in management meetings, and in any professional setting where the auditor interacts with audit customers. Therefore, it is important to realize that an auditor's conduct is constantly being observed and evaluated. All internal auditors, from staff up to the manager level, should consider themselves to be representatives of the department and conduct themselves accordingly. Creating and maintaining positive impressions by audit customers will result in their favorable comments to other audit customers.

The following tips may prove helpful in marketing internal auditing on a one-on-one basis with organization personnel:

- ***Hosting an open house***. Inviting audit customers to the internal auditing department is an excellent way to informally market the auditors. The open house should encourage operating personnel from all areas of the organization to visit the audit facilities and ask questions. It should be informational and conducted in a friendly, relaxed atmosphere.

- ***Refocusing preaudit meetings***. The focus of preaudit meetings can also derive marketing benefits when used as a vehicle for explaining internal auditing functions, processes, and procedures. Much of the apprehension surrounding the start of an audit can be relieved and other audit services can be explained for future reference.

- ***Establishing advisory contacts***. An advisory contact within the internal auditing organization can be established for each major organizational discipline, such as accounting, manufacturing, purchasing, etc. This person becomes the focal contact for operating personnel whenever a related issue or question requires a response by internal auditing. Operating personnel favor this process because they can build a personal relationship with their contact, achieve faster resolution of issues, and place greater reliance on internal auditing as a point of reference.

Employ available advertising media. Several good advertising options are available to internal auditing departments who want to educate their customers concerning audit functions and responsibilities within an organization:

- ***Marketing brochures.*** Preparing written brochures or reference pamphlets is a clever way to market internal auditing. These brochures tend to remove much of the mystery surrounding what auditors do. They can include summaries of internal auditing's mission, responsibilities, objectives, organization chart, and reporting structure. Brochures can also include information on the audit process itself, including the process of closing reported audit findings, the treatment of deficiencies related to economy and efficiency of operations, and the short-term and long-term audit plan. The audit department may want to do a mass mailing of these brochures to the entire organization, or they can be distributed individually (i.e., during audits, management meetings, etc.). See Exhibit 3.2 for a generic presentation of sample topics to be included in an audit brochure.

Exhibit 3.2
Internal Auditing Brochure
Partnering for Success

Internal auditing's charter: The audit charter or a summarized mission statement can be included to describe their purpose, authority, and responsibilities to the organization.

Description of staff and management: A brief description of the professional background and accomplishments of the audit staff and management may be included.

Description of audit duties and services: A description of the specific duties and services performed by auditors can be included, such as:

1. Scheduled audits.
2. Audit follow-ups.
3. Consulting reviews.
4. Project teams.

Endorsements: Executive management may agree to include a personal endorsement in the brochure to demonstrate their support for the internal auditing function.

Questions/answers: Commonly asked questions with their applicable answers may be included to provide a conversational way of addressing audit customer concerns.

- ***Newsletters/internal publications.*** Newsletters and other internal publications may be well-received by audit customers who find news articles interesting and informative. In addition, stories may be light in tone and anecdotal in nature in order to provide a human look at auditors. Audit customers may develop more empathy for internal auditors when they gain a better understanding of the common difficulties they face.

- ***Direct mail.*** In sending direct mail, the writer is personally communicating with audit customers. While there are numerous methods available in writing direct mail, here is a workable formula which covers all pertinent aspects:

  - *Get your audit customers' attention.* When appropriate, use headlines or key words in the opening paragraph to "hook" the attention of audit customers.
  - *Develop their interest.* State the reason for the letter and include related accomplishments.
  - *Demonstrate potential benefits.* State direct or indirect benefits to the customer, including quantifiable benefits whenever possible.
  - *Show your credibility.* Indicate credibility by offering a brief statement of educational or technical background.
  - *Suggest action.* Be clear and explicit as to what action is required by the customer.[6]

- ***Computerized advertising.*** Many large organizations are currently using internal, on-line computer systems to communicate between organizations. There are multiple types of systems available: some are designed for memos, letters, reports, or other written communication, while others are becoming more sophisticated, such as the newly developed Intranet systems, and include graphics, charts, portrait representation of sponsors, etc. This form of communication, further detailed in Exhibit 3.3, may prove to be a practical and conspicuous method of advertising internal auditing's services to the entire organization.

[6]Cohen, William A., *How to Make It Big As a Consultant* (New York, NY: American Management Association, 1991), pp. 21-23.

Exhibit 3.3
Communicating Through the Intranet

Many large commercial companies have recently taken a progressive attitude toward intercompany communication. A private net, or *Intranet* system, is now available on the market and serves a purpose similar to the World Wide Web, except that it limits access to company employees only. This intercompany system strictly controls access via "firewalls," software programs which effectively block public access. The Intranet can be used for basic information sharing between organizations. It is an inexpensive yet powerful alternative to other forms of internal communication.

Organizations now have an opportunity to "own" a page of their internal web. Internal auditing departments are also realizing the potential benefit and advertising advantages that the Intranet can afford. By obtaining a web page, an internal auditing department may recognize future payoffs:

Reaching customers. Internal auditing's web page can provide their customers with a description of internal auditing's goals and objectives, mission, current and future focus, and audit plan. The audit plan information can disclose the amount of audit resources set aside in anticipation of management-requested reviews or consultations. The web page can show annual audit statistics using graphics and charts. In addition, an organization chart can be included which would illustrate internal auditing's reporting structure and provide professional data (and even computerized portraits) about the audit management and staff.

Building goodwill and dispelling fear. Employees at all levels now have an opportunity to respond to the internal audit web page. The information on the web page is intended to eliminate the mystery surrounding internal audit and to promote interest in internal auditing's functions for all levels of company management and staff. By providing an easy-access vehicle to internal responses, management or other audit customers may find that requesting the auditor's assistance will be virtually painless and potentially profitable.

The Auditor's Marketable Assets

Internal auditors profess a variety of personal assets which have been developed through a combination of education, hard work, and experience. These assets include *reliability, independence, responsibility,* and *integrity,* but their most outstanding and marketable asset must be *adaptability.* Adaptability enables the internal auditor to accept new challenges and tailor the audit approach to meet the individual needs of audit customers, ultimately adding value to the organization. Although the concept of adding value seems to be somewhat overused in business circles, it precisely defines internal auditing's objective for the future. Adding value to the organization will inevitably add value to the auditing department.

Internal auditing's skills, education, accomplishments, professional activities, and other significant assets should be paraded in front of organization management as often as possible. Internal auditors are trained professionals and should be touted as such. The assets considered worthy of aggressive marketing include the internal auditor's:

- Accomplishments.
- Professionalism.
- Education, training, and experience.
- Audit philosophy: objectivity and independence.
- Leadership.

Accomplishments

An internal auditor's accomplishments are important assets to be marketed. They reflect the successes that internal auditors have already experienced and lend credibility to their processes and techniques.

Accomplishments may include company cost savings identified by auditors, special consultative reviews performed, or participation on project teams. These accomplishments should be well-publicized by audit management to keep key organization managers informed as to internal auditing's professional successes and achievements. Internal audit management may communicate these accomplishments during presentations to executive-level management, during meetings with operating management, in periodic progress reports, or in internal organization newsletters.

Professionalism

Professional behavior and mannerisms are marketable assets and essential elements in promoting internal auditors. Their professional training will be evident while performing audits, participating in organization meetings or conferences, or otherwise interfacing with managers. Because actions speak louder than words, professional behavior and a courteous manner of interacting with audit customers will be noticed and verbally communicated to other audit customers within the organization.

Personal integrity is a significant commodity, but difficult to publicize except through personal interaction. Auditors who display a firm yet understanding attitude during an audit will gain the confidence of management on all levels, which will help to establish and promote the auditing department as a group of professional individuals. In accordance with their professional disciplines, internal auditors must clearly demonstrate a sound code of ethics, set an example with a dedicated work ethic, and execute their responsibilities fairly, honestly, and without personal bias.

Education, Training, and Experience

Another powerful asset which can be marketed is the auditor's professional credentials, including skills, knowledge, and training. Section 540 of the *Standards for the Professional Practice of Internal Auditing (Standards)* states that "the director of internal auditing should establish a program for selecting and developing the human resources of the internal auditing department." Most auditing departments require auditors to hold a related undergraduate degree at a minimum. In addition, many auditors have earned graduate degrees and respected certifications (i.e., CPA, CIA, CISA, CMA, etc.). To ensure these certifications remain current, auditors must continue their educational process by attending classes or seminars to obtain continuing professional education (CPE) credits. Establishing minimum education requirements and providing ongoing training for internal auditors is proof of management's commitment to providing quality services to the organization.

Auditors may also be employed based on their specific knowledge and experience related to that industry and the operations which are audited. Organization management will have more respect for auditors who are conversant with and possess the necessary knowledge of the operation being reviewed; as a result, the auditors' recommendations and conclusions may be accepted more readily than they would be otherwise.

Audit Philosophy: Objectivity and Independence

Marketing an internal auditing department also means marketing their techniques, ethics, and philosophies to organization management. The professional attitude and views adopted by the audit manager will undoubtedly be emulated by staff auditors while performing audits. Such attitudes will influence the manner in which audit issues are addressed and audit customers are treated. Accordingly, when sensitivity, consistency, objectivity, and independence are employed throughout an audit, the support and confidence of organization managers will be earned, which will improve the auditing department's reputation and future marketability.

The internal auditor's objectivity and independence will be reflected during every phase of the audit process, especially in the final audit report. The conclusions presented in the audit report will indicate to the audit customer the reliability and honesty of the internal auditor. The audit report is the single most important document to be marketed by an auditor, and it should reflect the auditor's objectivity and independence. Therefore, an audit report can make or break the relationships formed with the audit customers during the review.

An auditor's credibility can be elevated to great heights or completely destroyed as a result of how accurate the final report presents the performance of the audit customer. The significance of issues and events discussed during the audit should be commensurate with what is ultimately reported. Inaccurate data, unnecessary comments, or condescending remarks could potentially damage internal auditing's credibility with organization management and subsequently result in distrust, a decrease in auditor support, and future animosity.

Leadership

Marketing internal auditors as leaders is an integral part of the development of audit customer relationships. Effective assumption of a leadership role can greatly improve an audit customer's perception of the internal auditor. The leadership qualities which have been attributed to successful auditors include intelligence, emotional maturity, initiative, communicative skills, confidence, and perceptiveness. Demonstrating these leadership qualities undoubtedly promotes the internal auditors' ability to wrestle with organization issues.[7]

Leadership is the art of influencing and stimulating performance. Effective leaders must be able to direct their available resources toward positive results. Some traits of an effective internal auditor in a leadership position include the following:

- Exhibiting confidence in subordinates.
- Encouraging a free exchange of ideas and team participation.
- Showing commitment to achieving organizational goals.
- Properly communicating project goals to subordinates.
- Understanding subordinates' problems, difficulties, and frustrations.
- Involving subordinates in the decision-making process.
- Motivating employees to peak performance.
- Establishing goals through group action rather than by command.
- Encouraging assimilation of the goals of the informal organization.
- Leading by example and avoiding imposed controls.[8]

The audit customer is the target *and* the beneficiary of the audit professional's experience, planning, and future activities. Internal auditors who are effective marketers have learned that developing customer relationships is key to their success. Developing these relationships hinges on the attributes and services that internal auditors can offer and communicate to their customers.[9] Direct action on the part of internal auditors is necessary to develop customer relationships, tailor their services to meet the needs of their customers, and continue their marketing program.

---

[7]Sawyer, Lawrence B., and Mortimer A. Dittenhofer, *Sawyer's Internal Auditing: The Practice of Modern Internal Auditing, 4th Edition* (Altamonte Springs, FL: The Institute of Internal Auditors, 1996), pp. 906-907.

[8]Ibid, pp. 1140-1141, 1146-1147.

[9]Connor, Richard A., and Jeffrey P. Davidson, *Marketing Your Consulting and Professional Services* (New York, NY: John Wiley & Sons, 1985), p. 6.

Chapter Summary

Marketing the accomplishments, expertise, knowledge, and other assets is a challenging and continuous task for audit management. Internal auditing's marketing program should be aggressive and dynamic in promoting their services to all levels of an organization's management and personnel. Most importantly, they must understand the goals and objectives of their customers in order to market the services which will be considered most valuable.

To ensure that organization personnel understand internal auditing's role and responsibility within the organization, a marketing program must conspicuously promote internal auditors and their key assets. Promotion of audit services may take several forms, such as written communication, formal presentations to organization management, or hosting an open house for all employees. There are numerous methods of effective marketing, ranging from sending out informative brochures to establishing a web site within an organization's Internet system. Whatever the marketing format, maintaining contact with audit customers is key to an extended and mutually beneficial relationship.

CHAPTER 4
HOW TO MARKET CONSULTING REVIEWS

Internal consulting is the ultimate application of the concept of partnering with management. A steady flow of requests from various levels of management is the best evidence of a constructive relationship between the internal audit function and the rest of the organization.

— Gil Courtemanche
Audit Management and Supervision

Challenges Facing Today's Managers

Organization managers have limited resources when it comes to solving a problem. They may consult their superiors to get a perspective of upper management's position. They may even solicit opinions from their staff to find out what concerns are paramount to their performance. However, when it comes to deciding upon a course of action, managers may not be satisfied that they understand all of their options and what each will mean when implemented.

Where organization managers once opted to bring in outside consultants to solve their business problems, more and more, managers are turning to internal auditing to perform specific reviews of operations when problems or deficiencies are identified or suspected. Hence, internal consulting is becoming synonymous with the concept of *partnering with management*.

Organization managers may be reluctant to employ a professional consultant for fear of incurring substantial costs or exposing sensitive organization information to an outsider. Internal auditing's consulting services are attractive to organization managers who need help in resolving internal issues or problems but do not have the necessary resources or manpower to accomplish the task.

A manager's primary goal is to provide an excellent quality product or service at a reasonable price to the customer while maintaining profitability for the organization. Accomplishment of this broadly stated goal is constantly challenged by internal and external factors:

- Operating budgets must be reduced while increasing the profit margin.
- Productivity must be increased while reducing manpower.
- A high standard of customer service must be maintained at all times.
- Managers must stay abreast of the industry standards, especially their competitors' products and prices.
- Efficiency in operations and timeliness in meeting deadlines is essential.

In order to successfully market services that will be useful, internal auditors must obtain a broad understanding of the needs and goals of their audit customers. In assessing the services they can offer to their audit customers, internal auditors should begin by asking the question, "How can internal auditing effectively assist organization managers in achieving their goals and objectives?"

Creating Marketing Opportunities

A consultant can be anyone who provides professional or semiprofessional advice or services in return for compensation. Internal auditors acting as consultants can assist organization managers by appraising the economy of their operations and the organization's method of providing ongoing quality control and process improvements. Moreover, internal auditors are trained to protect the organization's interests, which may relieve concerns managers may have about sensitive or privileged data being improperly exposed.

What makes an outstanding consultant? According to William A. Cohen, author of *How to Make it Big As a Consultant,* there are seven important attributes of an outstanding consultant:

1. ***Bedside manner:*** developing a professional rapport with the audit customer.
2. ***The ability to diagnose problems:*** understanding and correctly diagnosing the problem.
3. ***The ability to find solutions:*** identifying feasible alternatives for problem solving.
4. ***Technical expertise and knowledge:*** the consultant's background, experience, and knowledge.

5. ***Communication skills:*** being able to effectively communicate with the audit customer to understand their expectations.
6. ***Marketing and selling ability:*** learning to be a good marketer and salesperson.
7. ***Management skills:*** managing the project effectively.

To briefly summarize these attributes, we could say that the essential elements of being an outstanding consultant include having the necessary communication skills, both written and oral; being able to interact effectively with others; and having the technical expertise needed to perform consulting functions. Understanding what is needed will help internal auditors (as potential consultants) to master these concepts and increase their effectiveness.[1]

An internal auditor's consulting expertise may be requested for a variety of reasons:

- To provide input during the reengineering or reorganizing of a process or operational system which has become obsolete, useless, or otherwise lacks value to the organization.
- To examine current operations and recommend ways to improve economy and efficiency, productivity, or profitability.
- To assist management in making critical business decisions (i.e., making major purchases, changing accounting methodologies, consolidating operations).
- To identify missing or inadequate controls during the downsizing or reorganization of operations.
- To assist in an investigation of suspected fraud, misappropriation, or other wrongdoing.

Most consulting opportunities arise when management seeks out the advice of the internal auditors. However, internal auditing cannot always wait patiently and hope that management will come to them. Internal auditors who actively seek consulting opportunities will experience greater overall success as consultants.

[1]Cohen, William A., *How to Make It Big as a Consultant* (New York, NY: American Management Association, 1991), pp. 12-14.

Internal auditors should always be aware of and take advantage of the potential for marketing their services to management. When marketing a management-oriented service such as consulting, internal auditors should seek to maximize their opportunities. Such opportunities may occur:

- During a regular audit.
- During management meetings.
- In response to organization or industry events.

Marketing opportunities may be unanticipated, such as an impromptu meeting or a chance encounter with operating personnel. Other opportunities, however, must be planned and scheduled. In short, there are both direct and indirect methods to market internal auditing in their capacity as consultants. To *directly* market internal auditors as consultants and sell their services to management, the following methods may be employed:

- Direct correspondence.
- Scheduled manager meetings.
- Meetings during audits.

Indirect marketing methods should also be part of a long-term marketing program. These methods should generally be employed over a period of time to be truly effective. To *indirectly* market internal auditors as consultants, the following methods may be employed:

- Sending out audit newsletters to personnel within the organization.
- Training/teaching organization-sponsored courses and seminars.
- Joining and being active in company-sponsored organizations.
- Writing articles for organization-sponsored newspapers.
- Speaking before company personnel.

Each direct and indirect method are examined as follows:

Direct correspondence. Direct correspondence may take several forms, such as brochures or letters of intent. For example, a letter of intent may be distributed to all major organization heads explaining internal auditing's focus on consulting projects. The internal auditors may wish to follow-up this letter after one or two weeks to gauge management's reaction, solicit any concerns, or simply to answer any questions. See sample letter in Exhibit 4.1.

Exhibit 4.1
Sample Letter Promoting Audit Services

To: Major Organization Heads

From: Director of Internal Auditing

Subject: Audit Services

It has come to our attention that many company staff are unaware of the consultative services offered by the internal auditing department. Because of the recent company effort to reduce expenses, our department is modifying our audit focus to more closely correspond to management's objectives. While we will still be conducting our required compliance reviews, we are also expanding our services to include consultative reviews, which are discretionary and generally requested by company management. We recommend that these reviews focus on the economy and efficiency of operations, streamlining business processes, or examining the potential outcomes of complex decision-making processes.

Our department currently consists of ten staff members in addition to two clerical staff and myself. We are divided into two main teams: operational and information systems. Each team is made up of a supervisor and various levels of staff. This configuration is key in allowing us to review every facet of company business.

Our staff members possess undergraduate business degrees, and many have graduate degrees and related certifications. In addition, our staff members have proven experience in this industry, and many were hired from within the company based on their outstanding performance records.

Several staff members have already participated on project teams within the company and have led consulting projects for company managers. Based on our staff's knowledge of the industry and this company, we believe that internal auditing is well-equipped to handle consultative reviews. Our recent accomplishments also indicate that internal auditing can play a major role in such efforts, and we believe that we can make additional contributions in the future.

Our department has allocated a large percentage of our annual audit budget to assist company management in these types of projects. All requests will be given proper consideration. Please contact me in the event that you believe our department can be of assistance to your organization in any way.

Scheduled manager meetings. Request a separate meeting with each major organization head to personally explain internal auditing's intention to offer their services as consultants. Solicit concerns or offer to provide internal audit assistance as appropriate. If upcoming issues with potentially negative consequences are already known by internal auditing, this is a good time to discuss those issues with the responsible manager. The questionnaire in Exhibit 4.2 may also apply to these meetings.

Meetings during audits. During regularly scheduled audits, the internal auditor should plan to meet with the organization manager and upper-level staff to solicit concerns relating to the audit focus. Offer to allocate a portion of the audit budget toward investigating those concerns. A standard questionnaire may also be employed at this time to provoke and detect any underlying issues. The questionnaire illustrated in Exhibit 4.2 is designed to obtain both general and specific information directly pertaining to many consulting projects.

Exhibit 4.2
Management Questionnaire

General

1. What problem needs solving?
2. Precisely what do you expect to glean from my participation in this project?
3. How will you know if your objectives were properly met?
4. Are there any issues of particular significance or sensitivity which should be considered?
5. Who are the main points of contact?
6. Will a backup contact be available?
7. What authority does each player have?

Specific

1. What are the inherent risks associated with functions being audited? What are the most significant risks of your organization?

Exhibit 4.2 (Cont.)

2. How do you exercise control over your organization? What control reports do you receive from your own people?

3. How is the organization's performance measured by management and its customers?

4. What standards have you set for your own employees? How do you evaluate their performance?

5. What is the employee turnover rate?

6. How do you set priorities for your work?

7. In what areas of your controllable overhead budget do you feel cost savings may be possible?

8. What is the extent and nature of your backlog?

9. What organizations do you interface with? What kind of feedback do you get from them?

10. What are your annual objectives as dictated by upper management? How have you accomplished (or do you plan to accomplish) these objectives?

11. What reports do you prepare for your own management? How often?

12. What are your concerns associated with functions being audited? What areas do you think need the most attention?

13. Where do you feel economy and efficiency of operations could best be realized?

14. Do you have concerns that non-value added tasks are being performed?

15. Does your organization strive to improve their quality of performance? How is this documented and measured?

16. Is computerization provided to enhance effectiveness and efficiency of operations? Are steps taken to ensure potential automation is identified at every level?

Sending out audit newsletters to company personnel. The purpose of a newsletter is to dispense news of interest and value to potential audit customers. Newsletters promote internal auditing services by reminding audit customers of their availability.

Training/teaching organization-sponsored courses and seminars. Teaching courses or seminars must naturally pertain to the internal auditor's area of expertise and may form the basis for outside professional relationships.

Joining and being active in company-sponsored associations. Participation in company-sponsored organizations lends internal auditors more credibility. In addition, professional associations are excellent for making future contacts. Internal auditors can promote their consulting role in a relaxed, conversational atmosphere. Organizations, both professional and social, can also be a good basis for building long-term relationships.

Writing articles for organization-sponsored newspapers. Articles must be valuable, interesting, informative, and should pertain to the type of consulting internal auditors can do. Articles may also contain comments resulting from the auditor's expertise in the field.[2]

Speaking before company personnel. An excellent way of building a reputation as a consultant is to address company-related issues in-house in the form of lectures or speeches.[3] Addressing issues in this manner promotes the auditor as an expert on the subject, which may be the best vehicle for arousing the interest of known or potential audit customers.

Selling Reviews of Economy and Efficiency

Internal auditors have much to contribute to management's objective of employing economy and efficiency. Section 340 of the *Standards* charges internal auditors with the responsibility of appraising the economy and efficiency with which resources are employed. In other words, internal auditors are required to determine whether operations are performed in the best and least expensive manner possible while protecting and controlling assets and resources.

---

[2]Ibid, pp. 67-69.
[3]Ibid, pp. 38-56.

As a marketing tool, recommending ways to improve the economy and efficiency of operations earns more praise for internal auditors than any other. Internal auditors are professionally trained to systematically expose inefficiency and waste. In addition, they are independent assessors of systems and processes. Therefore, they have no ownership of the process under observation and are able to make a fair assessment of its value without conflict of interest.

Internal auditors and organization managers alike realize that deploying organization assets in an efficient and useful manner is key to the ongoing success of any organization. This marketing tool is extremely well-accepted by management as it serves to directly benefit their operation with measurable improvements, in most cases. Since the vast majority of economy and efficiency issues can be quantified in terms of dollar savings, management is much more likely to implement suggested recommendations.

Finding ways to ensure that organizations operate using the most economic and efficient methods can be an overwhelming task. Managers are constantly looking for ways to improve their operations to achieve greater productivity and profits for the organization. Hence, the auditor must use ingenuity and creativity in identifying the processes or operational areas for which improvement will result in the highest payback to management. The most likely processes will have a direct impact on time, cost, customer satisfaction, and/or productivity. Hence, issues or deficiencies which compromise the economy and efficiency of operations predominantly embody the following:

- Underutilized organization facilities.
- Nonproductive work.
- Procedures which are not cost justified.
- Overstaffing or understaffing.
- Inefficient use of organization funds.

Consider the following examples of internal auditors recommending ways to economize their organization's operations:

Example 1: Consolidating Facilities

A large company with a significant number of warehouse and office facilities is currently downsizing and is attempting to consolidate the remaining organizations into fewer facilities. As a result of the downsizing, redundancies exist within the organizations, such as company material which is housed in various warehouse facilities. Most of the company facilities are leased, and, while early termination of a lease is not always desirable and may result in contract penalties, these penalties may be more palatable than continuing lease payments. Therefore, executive management has tasked middle managers with consolidating operations as quickly and as cost effectively as possible.

Poor utilization of office or warehouse space results in a higher allocation of company overhead, ultimately affecting the company's profitability. An auditor reviewing this situation from a cost/benefit standpoint could feasibly quantify the cost of inadequate utilization **by calculating the unused square footage in existing facilities and applying it to the overhead rate.** The auditor could also review and evaluate management's proposed plan to consolidate operations, the monetary penalty involved in terminating leases early, and the cost and time frame for moving the various organizations into their new spaces. These factors could be compared against the long-term benefit to the company of consolidating operations.

Example 2: Maximizing Earnings Potential

A company maintains a bank account with a substantial cash balance (approximately $30 million). The funds are maintained in a low-yield account in anticipation that they will require immediate distribution at some point in the future for tax purposes. A small portion of the funds (approximately $5 million) are invested daily by an investment agency in overnight funds, which has earned a return of $127,000 in nine months (netting approximately .57%).

An internal auditor performing a review of this organization could suggest that **the funds be turned over to an investment agency who**

would manage and invest all available funds in short-term, high-yield investments. At an investment rate averaging 6%, these funds could be earning at least $1.8 million in the first year ($30 million x .06), compounding and increasing each year thereafter. By properly investing these funds, the organization could realize significant capital gains.

It is sometimes necessary to use creative means to identify potential areas of savings. Internal auditors are likely to target their principal process candidates by using one or more of the following procedures:

- ***Evaluation of critical processes.*** Identifying the critical processes for review means that the internal auditor should fully understand management's concerns and objectives, the operational restrictions of the organization, and other key operating data which will be useful in assessing the organization's strengths and weaknesses.

- ***Appraisal of customer satisfaction.*** If the organization is losing ground in the marketplace, they might be able to turn things around by improving the work processes for a specific product or service. An auditor can work with this concept by focusing on the elements that are specifically contributing to a decline in customer satisfaction.

- ***Identification of quality deficiencies.*** Typical warning signs of a work process in trouble include increases in errors, scrap, customer complaints, overtime, and employee turnover. An auditor should be alert to these signs that potential or actual problems are increasing in gravity.

- ***Investigation of process improvements.*** To get employees excited about process improvement, an auditor may select a process which is highly visible and for which improvements will make a big impact. Demonstrating how economy and efficiency analysis can largely affect an organization's productivity and profitability will also increase management's desire for similar reviews.

- ***Assessment of automation efforts.*** To understand the organization's status with respect to their development and automation of operations, the auditor should inspect their progress and make recommendations where further improvements are possible.

An organization considers its operations to be economical and efficient when the highest possible productivity level is achieved. According to Peter Drucker, the most desirable productivity level is achieved when an organization can provide the greatest output for the smallest effort.[4] The internal auditor's task of assisting management achieve their objectives includes providing useful feedback which will improve the productivity of current operations.

Productivity considers all factors which go into output and expresses them in relation to their effort. These factors include:

- ***Labor***, both of the worker and of the manager.
- ***Knowledge***, which is our most productive resource if properly applied, but also the most expensive and unproductive if misapplied.
- ***Time***, which is our most perishable resource.
- ***Product or process mix***, which is the balance between various combinations of the same resources.
- ***Organizational structure***, which relates to the balance among the various activities within the business.

Once productivity has been defined, the next step is to set objectives that take each of these factors into account.

By systematically approaching the issue of productivity and efficiency, the internal auditor will be able to review operations in a manner which will provide the most valuable end product to the customer — the company manager. Finding areas of waste or inefficiency will require the auditor to use creativity and investigative skills. In order to sell ideas to organization management, the internal auditor will have to rely on persuasion and compelling factual evidence.

If reviews that address the economy and efficiency improvements of a department are relatively new in the organization, the internal auditor may want to concentrate on a work process which is highly visible and would provide a payoff to the department as well as generate positive publicity and excitement elsewhere in the organization. The auditor's recommendations would have a high probability of success, benefit a large number of

---

[4]Drucker, Peter F., *Management: Tasks, Responsibilities, Practices* (New York, NY: Harper & Row Publishers, Inc., 1974), p. 68.

people in the organization, and link with the organization's process-improvement goals.[5]

There are an indefinite number of areas which can be probed once the auditor is turned loose to review the operations as a whole. Some audit concepts which may provoke additional questions and potentially lead to useful recommendations by the auditor are outlined in Exhibit 4.3. These questions delve into the operations from a management perspective and scrutinize some managerial decisions which can have distinct impacts on the bottom line.

Exhibit 4.3
Identifying Economy and Efficiency Deficiencies

In addition to the topics raised by the questionnaire in Exhibit 4.2, there are some key areas on which auditors can focus when beginning a review of economy and efficiency. The following questions and audit procedures may be used to isolate and analyze issues during such a review:

1. **Budget Allocations**

   - How are management's budget allocations determined?
   - Are allocations allowed based on input from each affected manager or in another systematic manner (i.e., headcount, square footage of office space, production, etc.)?
   - Can management demonstrate significant discrepancies between allocations allowed and actual budget needed to effectively manage the department?

2. **Overhead**

   - How is management attempting to reduce their current overhead costs?
   - Are there obvious areas of waste that management admits could be reduced?

[5]Zenger, John H., Ed Musselwhite, Kathleen Hurson, and Craig Perrin, *Leading Teams: Mastering the New Role* (Illinois/New York: Irwin Professional Publishing, 1994), p. 146.

Exhibit 4.3 (Cont.)

- Is manager's budget inflated as a result of additional overhead costs which are pooled and allocated among various departments? Are these costs appropriate for the manager's department?

3. **Continuous Quality Improvement**

- Has management established specific objectives and goals for implementing a quality improvement plan?
- How does management know that operations or processes are improving in their quality, efficiency, effectiveness, etc.?
- Are benchmarking procedures used for measuring performance?
- Are benchmarks based on company standards, industry standards, time standards, other?
- Does management monitor this process periodically?
- Are the results reported to upper management, and how often?
- Does the department receive input from outside sources, such as other managers (complaints or appreciation), customers (complaints or appreciation), or upper management (commendations, monetary awards, dissatisfaction, demotions)?
- How is corrective action accomplished?

4. **Automation and Duplication of Procedures**

A. What is management's attitude toward computers and automation?

- Does management avoid updating department with state-of-the-art techniques?
- Does management resist change in general?
- Does management purposely try to operate without automated procedures?
- Is management open to new ideas and constantly looking for ways to improve operations?

Exhibit 4.3 (Cont.)

- Does management have the "we've always done it that way" philosophy?

B. Review flowcharts or other documentation to obtain a thorough understanding of the processes for review. Review in detail each task that is included in the process. Analyze the value and status of each task by answering the following questions:

- Is task manually performed or an automated process?
  - If manual, does task provide value to overall process or operation?
  - Is task antiquated?
  - Was the same task performed when the company operated at a lower production level?
  - Has one employee always performed this task (or for a long time)?
  - Does this employee feel a distinct ownership of the task?

- Rank each task for level of importance:
  - What is the risk of error for each task?
  - What is the risk of untimeliness for each task?
  - What other operations could be affected by these risks?
  - Does a financial risk exist for the company as a result of these risks?

- What are the significant manual tasks and how often are they performed?
  - How many employees are dedicated to performing these tasks?
  - How many man-hours are required to perform these tasks?
  - What is the company cost to perform these tasks?
  - Could any of these tasks be candidates for automation?

Exhibit 4.3 (Cont.)

- Analyze the time spent performing manual tasks versus automated processes:
  - How much time is spent in manual operations (calculate man-hours by wages)?
  - How much time is utilized by automated processes or other computer usage (calculate cost of computerized operations)?
  - Compare both to the operational activity level (output in terms of dollars).
  - Is the amount of computer usage commensurate with the operational activity level?

- Review all tasks (manual and computerized) for task duplication:
  - Are there manual and computerized tasks which provide the same output?
  - Based on analysis of flowcharts, were non-value-added tasks identified?
  - Do wasted or unnecessary resources exist?

- Interview each employee and the corresponding manager:
  - Identify each employee's primary responsibility and the amount of time devoted to that task.
  - Identify subordinate tasks and their corresponding time requirements.
  - Ascertain whether individuals performing the same task overlap in their scope of work. Find out if each is aware of the scope of work performed by the other.
  - Review any cross-training techniques being implemented.

5. Resource Utilization

- Look for wasted time resulting from:
  - Underutilization of employee time.

Exhibit 4.3 (Cont.)

- Timing requirement of tasks which keep employee busy during peek times yet do not provide employee with enough work on a continuous basis.

- Compare responses to written job descriptions or descriptions on file with Human Resources:
  - Identify obvious deviations. Determine through this comparison whether the amount of time devoted to this task(s) is adequate.
  - Look for poorly utilized employee time:
    - Do employees leave on time each day?
    - Do employees take all possible breaks?
    - Do employees appear to be productive?

6. Policies and Procedures

Examine organization's policies and procedures for relevance, viability, and good sense:

- Is the date on the policy and procedure manual current?
- Are updates included, properly filed, and tracked to ensure completeness?
- Does it contain policies which do not pertain to current operations?
- Is it a "living" document, constantly changing to meet the needs of the organization?
- Does it contain outdated procedures which are no longer performed?
- Are the current procedures documented and relevant?
- Do these procedures make sense?
- Are the procedures approved by management?

Selling Reviews of Process Automation

The term *automation* conjures up images of vast assembly operations which run accurately and efficiently and require little human intervention. In fact, Peter Drucker states that the term *automation* was "coined in the late 1940s by a Ford Motor Company executive."[6] He goes on to explain that automation should not be viewed as simply an arrangement of machines; automation may work perfectly without any machines. For example, the abacus, a tool used by the Japanese and Chinese to perform complex calculations, is as fully advanced and sophisticated as any computer. It does not require machinery and advanced technology, but it still embodies the basic concept of automation.[7]

As Drucker so concisely summarizes, an automated process must satisfy four basic principles:

1. ***The entire process is seen as a system.*** There is no discernible beginning or end to the system, and every individual step is fully integrated into the entire process.

2. ***The system is based on the assumption that "phenomena of the natural universe fall into discernible patterns and can be routinized on the basis of a probability distribution."*** Translated, operational patterns within common processes may be identified and channeled into a workable procedure.

3. ***The system controls itself through feedback.*** The system recognizes errors and compensates with appropriate output or adjusts itself accordingly.

4. ***The human worker doesn't "work"; he programs.*** The worker makes decisions based on his judgment within the range of patterns the system is designed to handle. His tool is judgment rather than manual or even conceptual skill.[8]

For our purposes, understanding automation means understanding ways of translating work that is currently performed manually, or without the help

[6]Drucker, Peter F., *Management: Tasks, Responsibilities, Practices* (New York, NY: Harper & Row Publishers, Inc., 1974), p. 495.
[7]Ibid, p. 227.
[8]Ibid.

of machines or computers, into a streamlined process which is efficient, accurate, and, when possible, performed through computerization.

Automating operations is the first cousin of economizing operations and can also be marketed within the consulting realm. Recommending new and improved automation techniques will ultimately enhance the internal auditor's reputation and generate greater acceptance from organization management, who will view these suggestions favorably. Such recommendations may also result in frequent audit requests by management for assistance in achieving their goals of improving operations.

Exhibit 4.4 illustrates how an internal auditor made a significant contribution to her organization operations through a specific suggestion which resulted in the automation of a process and measurable time and cost savings for the organization.

Exhibit 4.4
Automating Currency Transaction Reports

A bank holding assets of approximately $500 million hired a new audit director. The director, whole background includes experience with much larger banking institutions, immediately began to scrutinize the numerous procedures that are manually performed. This bank, which was originally privately-owned, has slowly matured into a public institution, but automating their operations is only now being investigated.

Per the Bank Secrecy Act, the bank is required to file a Currency Transaction Report (CTR) for all cash transactions exceeding $10,000. Because the bank does not have a real-time computer system for their transactions, it is tedious and time-consuming to monitor these $10,000 transactions. It is especially difficult to track and monitor multiple inter-branch transactions made by the same person. This job has been performed by one bank employee, who spends 40 hours a week reviewing microfiche. She must review all 15 branches, tracking and monitoring transactions and looking for trends which might indicate illegal activities.

Exhibit 4.4 (Cont.)

The audit director knew that this task could be automated through the creation of on-line reports, since she had previously observed this process at other banking institutions. She approached the data processing specialist at the bank and suggested that such a report be generated. Once the report requirements were determined and programmed and the proper data was captured and retrieved, the computer system created a daily report which would disclose single and multiple $10,000 transactions by customers for all branches.

THE END RESULT: A job which previously required 40 hours per week to complete now requires only 10 hours per week, a net savings of 30 hours.

There is a wide variety of processes and systems that are excellent candidates for automation. As auditors become accustomed to these processes, they will increase their ability to recognize situations which will effectively lend themselves to functional streamlining. Exhibit 4.5 provides examples of how operations can be automated and includes commonly accepted applications of automating techniques.

Exhibit 4.5
Suggested Techniques for Automating Operations

The following is a partial list of tasks and procedures that could be considered candidates for automation. Alternative techniques have also been included whenever possible.

1. **Recurring Techniques:** Automated systems are excellent for many transactions, especially those that are recurring (i.e., monthly payroll, expenses, etc.). When archaic manual systems of transaction input are perpetuated, alternatives for automating the transactions should be considered:

Exhibit 4.5 (Cont.)

- Swiping encoded bar-codes for instantaneous data update.
- Computer keystrokes or other programming data can instruct computer system to automatically post general ledger accounts, generate payables and receivables, cut and mail checks, etc.
- Automated payroll system with automatic payroll deposit.

2. **Databases:** When organizations require the maintenance of multiple records or files, the establishment of an automated database can result in significant savings in time and cost, such as in:
   - Maintaining vendor files and ratings.
   - Tracking inventories (i.e., manufacturing parts and tools, negotiable securities, company fleet, fixed assets, company-owned buildings, etc.).
   - Maintaining employee files.
   - Qualifying customers for new business.
   - Providing customer service (i.e., accessing customer accounts).
   - Establishing and maintaining customer base.
   - Preparing monthly transaction reports.
   - Corresponding with vendors and customers.

3. **Spreadsheets:** Organizations may have a need to maintain data on spreadsheets for ease of accessing financial information, such as:
   - Computing transactions.
   - Accounting entries.
   - General ledger activity.
   - Flowdown to financial statements.

4. **Reporting:** Companies may require their organizations to prepare and submit periodic reports which summarize activities and productivity, such as:
   - Transaction, production, or activity reports.
   - Operational status (i.e., headcount or manpower base) reports.
   - Capital gains/losses or profit/loss reports.
   - Current and projected backlog of activity.
   - Expense comparisons.

Exhibit 4.5 (Cont.)

5. **Manual Logs:** With automation, manual logs become obsolete. Automated logs may now be used for:
   - Tracking transactions.
   - Listing transactions errors which require resolution.
   - Listing the status of errors.
   - Obtaining approval signatures.
   - Updating logs in a timely manner.

6. **Authorizations:** Required approvals or authorizations which were previously manual can now be obtained via computer. Computerized signatures can be programmed for specific documents. This method of obtaining required approvals will significantly reduce wasted time and the cost to transport documents between individuals for signatures.

7. **Data Transmission:** Intercompany computer software and modems can now be used to electronically submit data between departments. Some examples of this include:

   - Design engineers can produce engineering drawings and submit them to the Production Department for their review and input. Once revisions are complete, the drawings can be submitted to the Quality Assurance Department, and so on, until the drawings are accepted by all departments involved in the engineering process. This system would result in significant savings in time and cost, which will result in a lower cost of production.

   - Audit reports can be sent to cognizant managers for their preliminary review and comments prior to final issuance.

   - Monthly, quarterly, and annual financial statements can be submitted to company managers for their review and comments prior to closing the books. On-line adjustments to the statement totals may be made in a fraction of the original time required.

Exhibit 4.5 (Cont.)

9. **Communication:** Individuals can communicate with each other rapidly by using internal mail systems (i.e., E-mail) and telephone message software.

10. **Specialized Software:** Depending on the organization's needs and industry requirements, specialized software may be available to meet their specific needs, such as:
    - Engineering design.
    - Architectural design.
    - Diagramming and planning.
    - Inventory maintenance.
    - Flowcharting.
    - Accounting (i.e., general ledger and financial statements).
    - General business.
    - Business development.

Selling Reviews of Control Environments

In response to the economic downturn of the early 1990s, many organizations were required to reassess their financial needs in terms of manpower and related materials. To maintain their competitive edge, some were forced to reduce expenses and overhead, including human resources. Unfortunately, an unwelcome by-product of resource consolidation can be a reduction or loss of key internal controls, which can result in risk or damage to internal control structures.

In response to this situation, internal auditors are in a unique position to market their skills to managers who may be concerned with the consequences resulting from a loss of key controls. Internal auditors can effectively assist management in determining which controls can be discontinued without risking or compromising the quality of the organization's product or service.

Any loss or reduction of controls could result in deficiencies or weaknesses that could potentially lead to fraud, errors, or other misrepresentations. Reviews of control structures have always been the backbone of traditional audits. However, in the scenario described above, internal auditors should review the control environments to differentiate essential controls from those which are dispensable.

Peter F. Drucker, a preeminent author of business and management concepts and practices, poses the question, "How can *controls* [which have been improved over time] give better *control* to management?"[9] Webster defines a control as "a mechanism used to regulate or guide the operation of a system." While sometimes used interchangeably, "controls" should not be confused with "control." Establishing many *controls* will not necessarily ensure that more *control* over the process or system will be attained. Drucker further implies that each word has a very different meaning and implication:

> "The synonyms for *controls* are measurement and information; the synonym for *control* is direction. Controls pertain to means, control to an end. Controls deal with facts and the events of the past; control deals with expectations of the future. Controls are analytical, concerned with what was and is; control is normative and concerned with what ought to be."[10]

Marketing internal audit's expertise in assessing control environments is key. When undertaking a review of controls, it is helpful to approach the importance of each control in terms of risk. Perceived or actual risk will dictate whether the control is necessary or extraneous. Internal auditing is in a good position to market this service when they identify an organization that has experienced significant:

- Staffing changes.
- Structural or organizational changes.
- Headcount reductions.

Such organizational changes should be an immediate indication to internal auditing that potential control problems are likely. In order to promptly react to these organizational needs, internal auditing should closely monitor organizational activities.

---

[9]Drucker, Peter F., *Management: Tasks, Responsibilities, Practices* (New York, NY: Harper & Row Publishers, Inc., 1974), pp. 494-495.
[10]Ibid.

Once a need has been identified, internal auditing should directly approach responsible organization management with a suggestion to initiate a review of controls. This review may be in the form of a consulting exercise rather than a regular control review. Management will likely be more open and willing to host a consultative review rather than take the chance of being audited later.

When selling reviews of control environment, internal auditors should indicate to their potential audit customers their methodology in identifying inadequate control environments, as in the following procedures:

Identifying key controls. Internal auditors evaluate controls for functionality, feasibility, and value. They are focusing on the related risk in terms of product quality, cost, customer relations, timeliness, profitability, and other factors which may have significant business impacts. When the value of a control is in question, the internal auditor should employ a systematic method of determining its importance and usefulness. The following questions should be answered in order to properly determine whether a control should be discontinued:

1. What event does the control ensure will occur?
2. What is the risk of discontinuing or modifying the control?
3. Can the risk be quantified?
4. What is the exposure?
5. Does the existence of the control benefit the financial statements?
6. Does removal of the control compromise the financial statements?
7. What are the benefits of discontinuing or modifying the control?
8. Can the benefits be quantified?

The answers to these questions should indicate whether the control in question adds value to the process. Internal auditors should take care in discriminating between high priority controls and those having only cosmetic effects on operations. By analyzing controls in terms of risk, the operations with the highest risk to the organization will become apparent and should be prioritized. In addition, risks without mitigating controls will also be detected and assessed for their potential effect on the operation.

Controls must be questioned when their purpose is ambiguous or unknown. Many unnecessary controls may be routinely performed but may not contribute or add value to the process or activity. Instead, unneeded controls may be draining organization resources. Thorough analysis should be performed to determine their status and worth.

Applying appropriate criteria. Controls are a means to an end. In order to have control over an operational system, effective controls must be developed. Internal auditors should apply the following criteria in determining the value of each control:

- ***Controls must be economical.*** The fewer controls needed, the more effective they will be. Large quantities of controls will not ensure greater control but more confusion. In addition, adding many unnecessary controls may impact profitability by increasing the cost of doing business.

- ***Controls must be meaningful.*** The events to be controlled must play a significant role in the operation of the organization. Controls should be related to the key objectives and priorities within the business environment.

- ***Controls must be appropriate.*** It is critical that business managers carefully select the most appropriate controls on which to focus their time, attention, and resources. These controls will become the grounds for effective action by managers and their staff.

- ***Controls must be timely.*** Business managers must apply the appropriate periods of time to controls in order to attain the desired results which will enable them to achieve their objectives. They must also pay attention to the measurement of results at their crucial moments in time.

- ***Controls must be simple.*** Complicated controls do not work. They often misdirect attention from what is to be controlled to the mechanics of the control itself. If learning the control and what its measurement means must be taught, then the control is useless.

- ***Controls must be operational.*** The control measurement must result in a form that is suitable, understandable, and usable by the recipient. In addition, the outcome of the control must be communicated to the individual who is responsible for taking controlling action.[11]

---

[11]Ibid, pp. 498-505.

Internal auditors who market consultative reviews of internal controls as another service to organization managers will effectively fulfill an important need. After their initial assessment, subsequent reviews may be appropriately scheduled to provide assurance that recommendations were properly implemented. The next generation of controls will also require distinct reevaluation of organization objectives. These and subsequent control reviews will provide internal auditors with the recognition they desire and will demonstrate that they are willing participants on management's organization team.

Benefits and Risks of Partnering with Management

An organization and its personnel realize both financial and administrative benefits from enlisting the auditor's services. Clearly, organization managers can take advantage of the auditor's resources without dedicating their own staff and budget for the task, which will result in an organizational cost savings. Since internal auditors have the benefit of being able to oversee a significant cross-section of the organization, they may be able to apply this broad-based knowledge to interrelated company operations. Some internal auditors may also be able to effectively apply whatever insight they have gained from past experiences at other organizations.

These attributes will serve to benefit management by providing a broader perspective of the problem or issue in question. When organization management and internal auditors work in cooperation, specific rules for audit performance may be established at the outset of the project, including:

- Content and scope of the review.
- Specific conditions and guidelines governing review.
- Criteria or standards for performance.
- Grounds for unacceptable results.
- Method of reporting results and report distribution.

Internal auditing should apply criticality to the management requests received when evaluating them for consistency with their audit charter. In addition, internal auditing should assess the risk element involved, both to the organization and to themselves. Requests should be rejected in the event they violate internal auditing's charter or professional ethics, are unreasonable in nature, or in any way compromise internal auditing's independence or objectivity.

Performing management-requested reviews involves some distinct hurdles for internal auditors to overcome. Gil Courtemanche, author of *Audit Management and Supervision*, stated:

> "The special challenge of internal consulting is to resist undue management influence that might interfere with the delivery of a quality product. Accordingly, the audit department must exercise good judgment in accepting internal consulting engagements and should decline (or retire from) any engagement where conditions do not permit doing a good, professional job."[12]

Success in internal consulting is achieved when company management frequently requests the services of internal auditing. The frequency of internal consulting requests received is a clear indication of the relationship established between internal auditing and management. Operating management as the audit requester wants to be treated as the client and to have its legitimate interests protected. Courtemanche goes on to say that "audit departments with a high degree of organizational status receive frequent requests for assistance...and it is precisely that status which enables them to resist undue influence upon their work."[13]

Internal consulting provides some self-actualizing benefits to internal auditors as well. Acting as internal consultants allows auditors to be creative and innovative in their thinking and in their assessment of an activity or problem. It gives them a feeling of making a separate contribution to the health of their organization. Moreover, the knowledge gleaned through consulting activities will ultimately contribute to the auditors' technical expertise and understanding of those activities, which will make them better auditors in the long run.[14]

An improvement in internal auditing's image will enable them to become increasingly more visible to organization management. In addition, internal consulting will provide greater opportunities for internal auditing staff to interact with executive management. Internal auditors who, through their internal consulting activities, are able to make constructive, practical sug-

---

[12]Courtemanche, Gil, *Audit Management and Supervision* (New York, NY: John Wiley & Sons, 1989), p. 26.

[13]Ibid, p. 26,128.

[14]Ibid, p. 4.

gestions for controlling or decreasing costs may provide legitimate reasons for being spared from subsequent budget cuts and layoffs.[15]

Although internal auditors may switch hit by performing both auditing and consulting activities, there are some distinct theoretical and conceptual differences between the two, as illustrated in Exhibit 4.6 on the following page.

A Word of Caution

Standard 100 reiterates auditors' responsibility to employ independence and objectivity during their reviews. This requirement may seem simplistic when performing compliance reviews, but there are some distinct conflicts that must be addressed during internal consulting activities.

The question of audit independence must be assessed at the level of the audit engagement. Courtemanche teaches us that, for management-requested reviews, independence may be considered acceptable if the nature and circumstances of the audit engagement:

- Advocate corporate objectives.
- Support executive management's needs and ambitions.
- Provide quality of audit work.
- Comply with appropriate ethics and standards required of the internal auditing profession.
- Do not hinder audit performance and other audit priorities.

Assuming these five conditions are satisfactorily met, the working relationship between the internal auditor and the responsible manager should be harmonious and productive. The auditor's findings and recommendations will be accepted and received with greater cooperation, since these types of reviews are usually initiated by management.[16]

Auditors who consult with organization management must continually exercise discerning judgment as to whether the particular activity they have been asked to perform will in any way provoke a future conflict of interest. For example, if auditors have been requested to study and recommend a new accounting software, they may later be put in a position of evaluating

---

[15]Ibid. p. 3.

[16]Ibid, pp. 112-113.

Exhibit 4.6
Internal Auditing versus Consulting

Internal Auditing...	Internal Consulting...
is a post-review.	is ongoing, real-time advising.
is based on past history.	is future-oriented, proactive involvement.
is geared toward controls and transactions.	is geared toward efficiency and issues.
is an independent appraisal of controls in place, through inspecting, verification, and certification.	is reviewing and providing technical advice and opinions on professional matters.
is performed independently according to a preconceived plan.	is frequently performed as a team approach on a collaborative basis.
usually reports to audit committee or CEO.	reports to responsible manager requesting service
is part of a management directive, part of an audit program, legal, or ethical requirement, or in response to an impropriety.	responds to a call for help.
is more supervisory and reporting.	is more interactive and problem solving.
is designed to meet requirements of the audit committee.	is designed to meet the needs of the unit requesting help.

Adapted from *Business Management Auditing: Promotion of Consulting Auditing*, by Glen L. Gray and Maryann Jacobi Gray, published by The Institute of Internal Auditors, 1994, p. 19-22.

that decision as part of an audit. Therefore, consistent analysis must be exercised throughout the course of the review to ensure the auditors' actions are consistent with ethical and professional standards.[17]

Once a proven track record of consulting successes is established, organization management will begin to demand and expect a high quality of consulting expertise from the audit department. This accomplishment can actually become a liability to some audit departments in the form of an expectations risk. Meeting management's expectations may have impacts on staffing, budgeting, and scheduling, which in turn may prevent the audit department from performing its traditional auditing duties.

In addition, organization management may begin to expect internal auditing to accept even the most specialized consulting projects. In doing so, internal auditing would be forced to support this demand by providing training to their staff in these specialized areas, which again may impact their ability to complete their traditional auditing plan.[18] Exhibit 4.7 on the following page illustrates a similar scenario and how it was resolved by the internal auditor.

[17]Gray, Glen L., and Maryann Jacobi Gray, *Business Management Auditing: Promotion of Consulting Auditing* (Altamonte Springs, FL: The Institute of Internal Auditors Research Foundation, 1994), p. 51.

[18]Ibid, p. 50.

Exhibit 4.7
A Case Study of Cost Allocations: Their Pros and Cons

The vice president of finance contacted the director of internal auditing and requested an investigation of cost allocations used by the various companies within the corporation. This investigation would include a review of the current utilization rates used, past and currently scheduled commitments, and application methodologies. The vice president was interested in comparing the various philosophies and methodologies in order to identify the most outstanding approach and apply it to his own company. He also indicated that he did not know the amount of time this project would require.

The director of internal auditing assigned this project to a senior internal auditor, and he requested that she prepare a preliminary budget and projected time requirement for this review. Once the budget and time line were approved, the auditor began the project by contacting finance managers from the other companies and obtaining verbal information regarding cost allocations. Each manager's position and theory was carefully documented.

After examining all possible cost allocation options and reviewing the positive and negative consequences of each, the auditor's final conclusion was that there were several viable options from which the vice president could choose. However, she did not feel comfortable making a specific recommendation or endorsing a particular option because each option also included negative consequences. Both the negative and positive aspects were carefully reviewed by the vice president, since he is ultimately responsible for the decision. The auditor decided that, by remaining neutral and not making a specific recommendation, her objectivity was not impacted, and performing future audits of this area would not result in a potential conflict of interest.

After obtaining approval from the director of internal auditing, the auditor verbally conveyed the results of her review to the vice president. In addition, the auditor provided copies of specific documentation to indicate what procedures were performed and the outcome of each cost allocation method reviewed. The auditor prepared an internal memo for her audit file to document the reasons behind her decision not to issue a formal audit report.

Chapter Summary

Internal auditors are making a transition to becoming internal consultants for organization management, capable of providing services comparable to professional external consultants. By effectively marketing internal auditing's services, qualifications, and skills, managers are calling on the auditors more and more. As a result, these managers are realizing a financial savings plus gleaning a benefit from the auditor's knowledge of organization and industry.

Creativity may be internal auditors' most useful asset. This creativity is tested when auditors are recruited by company management to tackle complex assignments, such as identifying inefficiency and waste within the business operations. Every organization's primary goals are to increase customer satisfaction, decrease the cost of doing business, and increase product quality. Awareness of these goals will serve to improve the auditors' focus in concentrating on areas that organization management considers to be important.

Most importantly, consulting reviews can be considered an exercise in building goodwill. Internal auditors, acting as internal consultants, can further the reputation of their department and ensure similar requests in the future by conducting themselves in a professional manner, performing the review effectively, and by cautiously deferring to the manager's purpose and objectives.

CHAPTER 5 PARTICIPATING ON PROJECT TEAMS

The person that figures out how to harness the collective genius of his or her organization is going to blow the competition away.

— Walter B. Wriston
Former Citicorp/Citibank Chief Executive Officer

Why Employ Project Teams?

Until recently, problems emerging from everyday operations were typically assigned to one or two people who were considered to be the most knowledgeable in that area. Unfortunately, what usually resulted from such an arrangement was an inability to solve the problem. In the event the problem could be solved, finding a solution was inefficient, time consuming, and frequently unacceptable to management.

In response to this dilemma, management began to use a different approach, one that cut across organizational boundaries and included individuals who had the knowledge, responsibility, and ability to fix the problem. Thus, the *team concept* emerged.

The United States is only now beginning to take advantage of the fellowship and benefits created by teamwork. The American Society of Quality Control estimates that about 20 percent of the organizations in this country have implemented employee-managed teams, an overall increase in the trend toward team solutions. Although this number seems low, it still represents a significant improvement in the last 10 years (10 years ago, only about five percent of U.S. organizations were using teams for the purpose of continuous improvement). Unfortunately, only 20 percent of organizations are taking advantage of team-based problem-solving; 80 percent of our business enterprises have yet to take advantage of this powerful technique.[1]

---

[1]Berk, Joseph, and Susan Berk, *Total Quality Management* (New York, NY: Sterling Publishing Co, Inc., 1993), p. 96.

The use of project teams provides organization management with many benefits. Internal teams generally consist of personnel from all organizations and levels. Other teams may be formed at the request of customers or vendors who have specific objectives, such as joint audits or implementation of new procedures. Significant benefits may be derived from the diversity of backgrounds, expertise, and personalities of those selected to participate.

By utilizing the experience and strengths from each team member, the diversity of ideas will also be widened, providing a higher quality of output. Each team member possesses a unique interest in how the outcome affects the organization, which will help to shape the outcome of the project. In addition, when organization personnel are partnered with customer or vendor personnel, goodwill is promoted and built.

Project teams are able to address and delve into controversial or sensitive subjects which may have previously been restricted or discouraged by management. Suggestions or recommendations that result from team analysis are generally candid, independently developed, and geared toward improving the welfare of the organizations or groups involved. In short, the team concept has substantially proven itself to be a worthwhile investment in organization resources given its record of successes within its short period of existence.

How Does Internal Auditing Fit In?

In the past, management has been reluctant to include internal auditing in the team process for fear that "airing dirty laundry" will invite an unwanted audit. However, project teams are growing in popularity within many organizations. They are less threatening than traditional audits because they involve a variety of individuals with different backgrounds and objectives. By having internal auditors serve on such a team, it sends a message to management that internal auditing is interested in improving the organization's process, rather than just finding and reporting deficiencies.

Internal auditors bring a unique unity to the team by acting as impartial observers and making suggestions based on knowledge gained from exposure to other areas. Employees who work in one area may concentrate only on what is best for their area and lose sight of the big picture.

Internal auditors are able to cross departmental lines and make suggestions which may improve all areas of operation. Because of their status within the organization, internal auditors are also able to suggest operational improvements which may target several levels of management without fear of reprisal. As a result, the project sponsor is assured of being provided with a complete package of options. Once again, participation promotes internal auditors as willing contributors and team players.

Unfortunately, there are some distinct hazards for internal auditors as a result of team participation. Not all team members will consider an internal auditor's involvement in a favorable light and may find it difficult to accept the auditor as a willing and valuable participant. Auditees may fear that their candid response to questions may potentially result in audit findings. As a result, internal auditors may have to "sell" themselves to the other team members.

Another hazard must be considered at a later time when the subject group is being audited by the internal auditing department. Audit management should determine whether the auditor who participated on the project team should be excluded from future audits of that area to avoid any potential conflicts of interest.

Project Teams as a Marketing Tool

Participation on a project team is a good way for auditors to improve their reputation and status within their organization. As a marketing tool, auditors have a prime opportunity to *partner with organization management and their staff*. Securing internal auditor involvement in these teams is the biggest hurdle.

When the members of a project team are being selected and assembled, the team sponsor will likely consider candidates from within the organization who:

- Have influence over the performance of the review.
- Will be directly affected by the outcome of the project.
- Have specific experience which will benefit the project.
- Have authority or responsibility for implementing the suggestions resulting from the project.

The team sponsor may consider operating management, knowledgeable organization staff, internal auditors, or even external auditors, depending on the subject under review. In addition to the inherent disadvantages already discussed, internal auditors may not be selected for team participation if the team sponsor is unaware of their skills, technical expertise, and other related experiences. Thus, internal auditors must "market and sell" their wares to organization management by directly promoting their abilities and specific experience.

Internal auditors can increase their chances of participating on a project team through direct solicitation and marketing of their services. Effective marketing occurs when internal auditors openly communicate their willingness to partner with management and operating personnel on project teams. Internal auditors who demonstrate their technical knowledge of operations will be viable candidates for projects related to that area of expertise. The following methods have proven to be effective in marketing internal auditing's desire to participate on project teams:

- Designating audit specialists.
- Direct marketing by audit management.
- Monitoring organization activities.

Designating audit specialists. An auditing department can designate individual auditors as contacts, or "specialists," within the organization. Each audit specialist should be thoroughly trained to be proficient and knowledgeable concerning the activities and processes performed by their assigned organization. The organization should be made aware that they now have a specific point of contact within internal auditing. As organization members increase their interaction with their specialist, their comfort and confidence level will also increase. As opportunities for project teams occur, the organization will be more likely to consider including their resident audit specialist when forming project teams.

Having specialists within internal audit can benefit organizations in several ways:

- Anyone within that organization wishing to ask an audit-related question may speak directly with their assigned specialist, who is already knowledgeable in this area.
- Audit-related issues may be resolved quickly and efficiently by the specialist.

In addition, the internal auditing department will also benefit from this process:

- When organizational issues arise which require a team solution, the specialist can openly solicit his inclusion as a team member.
- The specialist will be able to keep his own audit management well-informed when related issues arise.
- The specialist will gain significant knowledge in his area of expertise.
- The specialist will build a professional, working relationship with the organization members, which will be helpful during audits, project teams, and other activities.

This process provides the auditees with direct access to problem-solving and builds goodwill between internal auditing and organization personnel. By advertising themselves as "resident experts" on a variety of subjects, internal auditors offer many potential benefits to the project team. Moreover, knowing that their audit specialist is available for inclusion on project teams will prompt organization management to utilize that expertise when appropriate.

Direct marketing by audit management. Being alert to opportunities to promote internal auditors as potential team players is essential. Candid and direct solicitation of their staff's services to organization management is necessary to create opportunities for team participation. This solicitation of internal auditing's expertise and desire to participate in team environments can be accomplished through:

- *Direct communication:* mass mailings or phone conversations.
- *Management meetings*: meetings with all responsible organization heads, meetings during regularly scheduled reviews, etc.
- *Presentations to executive management*: in conjunction with presentations of audit progress and annual audit plan status.

Monitoring organization activities. Party crashers are seldom appreciated, since their actions may discourage the trust and favor of other invited guests. However, if the party crashers come to the party bearing significant and valuable contributions, the other guests may be persuaded to overlook their shortcomings.

Internal auditors can apply this analogy to their marketing of project teams. Internal auditors may find that "crashing the party" enables them to increase their exposure and their chances of being included on project teams. They should request an opportunity to participate on project teams when they first learn that:

- A company problem has been identified.
- A project requiring team evaluation has been initiated.
- Management is in the process of forming a project team.

By now, audit management should understand organization management's goals and objectives. Furthermore, they should be conscious of management's reaction regarding audit intervention on company issues. Assuming that audit management is comfortable with their organization status and relationship with management, they should offer or request to be included in team activities when appropriate. This offer is an acceptable gesture if:

- The team's mission is consistent with internal auditing's responsibilities.
- No conflict of interest is discernible.

Management may respond to internal auditing's offer with either gratitude and appreciation or dread and apprehension. The worst-case scenario is that management could decline internal auditing's offer completely. However, considering the potential benefits to be gleaned from internal auditing's experience and company knowledge, and management's desire to maintain inter-company goodwill and show support for internal auditing, it is highly unlikely that such an offer would be rejected. Once management's confidence in internal auditing's abilities and team spirit begins to grow, internal auditors will be regularly invited to participate on project teams.

Marketing Creativity

Utilizing creative instincts is one of the internal auditor's most powerful marketing tools. Creativity is essential in developing the team's strategy for achieving their objectives within established task boundaries. As studied by Sawyer, creativity may be fostered by a variety of activities:

> ***Constructive discontent.*** When one believes that a practice exists which is superior to current practices, discontent emerges and initiates action.

Observation. When activities and operations are analyzed for weaknesses, improvements may be identified.

Combination. Existing concepts may be combined to form a better methodology.[2]

The internal auditor is expected to contribute knowledge, background, and professional opinions to the project team. As a result of past audit experience, the auditor is accustomed to recognizing his or her own instincts and following them through to their final resolution. In turn, the auditor may be able to teach and encourage other team members to follow their instincts in gathering and interpreting data. The key to the team's success will ultimately be measured by the quality and integrity of the data collected and how it is used in developing recommendations.

Sawyer tells us that creativity in modifying a process can be studied in terms of order, structure, and relation. When studying a process, the following questions may be asked:

Order pertains to change relating to time and space.

- What are the steps and phases of a process? Can they be enlarged or reduced? Can their timing be increased or decreased?
- Can the process be expanded? Can it be intensified, repeated, added to, or built up?
- What interactions occur? What is the cause and effect?

Structure pertains to differences.

- What group does the process fit into? Can it be adapted?
- What is its character? What are its properties?

Relation deals with similarities.

- Can the process be reversed?
- Can the process be rearranged?
- What combinations can be identified?

---

[2]Sawyer, Lawrence B., and Mortimer A. Dittenhofer, *Sawyer's Internal Auditing: The Practice of Modern Internal Auditing, 4th Edition* (Altamonte Springs, FL: The Institute of Internal Auditors, 1996), p. 907.

- What other alternatives are possible? What substitutes are available?
- Can the process be modified or changed? Can there be a change in meaning, purpose, use, and objective?[3]

Creativity should be encouraged within the established task boundaries. Setting task boundaries is a tool which defines the non-negotiable limits on the team's decision-making authority. Task boundaries establish the arena within which the team decides the specifics of performing a given task. The minimal non-negotiable boundaries within which the team has to operate may include the following categories:

- Organizational requirements.
- Quality requirements.
- Quantity requirements.
- Customer or stakeholder needs.
- Budgetary limitations.
- Space limitations.
- Technical limitations.
- Availability of resources.
- Key dates and deadlines.
- Regulations.

The team leader is responsible for identifying all critical task limitations to avoid setting up the team for potential failure. Once task boundaries have been established, subsequent changes must be properly justified.[4] Limits on creativity should conform with the restructured task boundaries.

Projects Suitable for Internal Auditors

Project teams are generally ad hoc, since they are formed at the discretion of the team sponsor. Teams are organized primarily for the purpose of evaluating a particular problem, process, or business activity, reengineering processes or procedures, or making recommendations for other operational

[3]Ibid, pp. 1107-1108.
[4]Zenger, John H., Ed Musselwhite, Kathleen Hurson, and Craig Perrin, *Leading Teams: Mastering the New Role* (Illinois/New York: Irwin Professional Publishing, 1994), pp. 79-80.

improvements. Internal auditors may appropriately be included on project teams which address specific management concerns such as:

- Streamlining operations.
- Conducting investigations.
- Identifying best practices.

Streamlining Operations

When project teams are formed for the purpose of streamlining operations, their task is to research and develop proposed operational changes or automation functions by:

- Helping the organization better understand their customer requirements in terms of quality, time, and cost.
- Streamlining business processes to initiate and sustain improvements.

Assume that a particular process has been identified by management as ineffective, and the team has been asked to find ways to improve the process, reduce the costs, etc. Developing a new process using the old process as a guideline requires an in-depth understanding of the process.

Internal auditors are proficient in systematically evaluating a process by first documenting, or mapping, the "as is" process. Once a process map has been developed to include all procedures, both formal and informal, the team can identify opportunities for improvement, such as redundancies, inconsistencies, needless complexities, or potential trouble spots.

As opportunities for improvement are identified, they can be prioritized in accordance with desired results, based on customer expectations, management expectations, company focus, or whatever the most appropriate criteria happens to be. The issues with the highest risk and most visibility should be investigated before cosmetic problems are considered.

Conducting Investigations

Investigations may evolve around suspected fraud or misappropriation, complex business decisions, or issues involving external customers or vendors. When teams are formed for these highly sensitive reviews, creativity will be the driving factor in providing a direction. Information in and of itself may not be enough to point the team in a useful direction. They will need to analyze their information in terms of internal needs and priorities, then decide on subsequent steps. As a rule, the more information the team knows about their organization and the issue under investigation, the better they will be able to assess the importance of the information they obtain.[5]

Some investigations are performed by internal control agencies upon request by responsible management. Internal auditing departments who routinely communicate with these control agencies may be more likely to be included in an investigation team. Such teams may be formed for the purpose of exposing a defalcation or fraud, identifying and validating internal corruption, or other covert investigations initiated by responsible management. As part of the team, internal auditors would be instrumental in acquiring necessary documents and providing an independent assessment of critical issues.

Identifying Best Practices

Rules and procedures can build up over the years in response to conditions that may no longer apply to the current company environment. Besides wasting time and money, they contribute to higher error rates. Correcting errors adds to costs. If the team can find ways to prevent errors from occurring in the first place, then significant amounts of money can be saved.

Project teams may be formed to assist management with future decision-making activities by seeking out and evaluating business alternatives for the purpose of:

- Identifying and minimizing non-value-added activities.
- Improving value-added activities.
- Implementing process-analysis-based improvements.

Organization management may consider internal auditors to be strong candidates for participation on a project team that will be identifying best practices. Internal auditors demonstrate discerning judgment, which is essential in identifying superior performers in the business environment.

[5]Sawyer, Lawrence B., and Mortimer A. Dittenhofer, *Sawyer's Internal Auditing: The Practice of Modern Internal Auditing, 4th Edition* (Altamonte Springs, FL: The Institute of Internal Auditors, 1996), p. 152-153.

One of the most popular reasons that organization managers form project teams is to research industry practices in order to incorporate proven methodologies used by superior performers. This practice, known as *benchmarking*, involves measuring products, services, or processes against those of recognized leaders to identify areas for improvement.

The purpose of using benchmarking techniques is to rank a group's performance relative to that of another considered to be superior in a given field. Once the techniques of the superior performer are identified, they can then be applied to the project team's organization. Because of the recent importance placed on teams performing benchmarking procedures (including a proper interpretation of their results and subsequent implementation), we have included guidelines for team benchmarking.

Using Benchmarking Techniques

When quality standards must be redefined or operational processes become ineffective or a hindrance to the overall operation, a practical method of identifying superior business techniques is to "benchmark" the process or system. Benchmarking brings about an awareness of external companies and their methodologies. This technique helps to improve quality and establish priorities leading to a competitive advantage.

Benchmarking is an extremely useful tool in giving management ideas of how to accomplish a task or process in less time, with better controls, or by spending less money. This process effectively challenges the business-as-usual syndrome and forces management to reexamine current business practices.

Benchmarking Benefits

As a member of a project team, an internal auditor may find that using benchmarking techniques will help identify alternative procedures which will be acceptable to organization management. Management's acceptance of team proposals is based on the fact that procedures recommended as a result of benchmarking already have assurances built-in to their performance. When superior performance strategies are emulated, the likelihood of success is simultaneously increased. In addition to these benefits, benchmarking:

- Teaches organization leaders how to compete.
- Improves organizational quality.

- Leads to lower cost positions.
- Creates buy-in for change.
- Exposes people to new ideas.
- Broadens the organization's operation perspective.
- Creates a culture open to new ideas.
- Serves as a catalyst for learning.
- Increases front-line employees' satisfaction through involvement, empowerment, and a sense of job ownership.
- Tests the rigor of internal operating targets.
- Overcomes front-line employees' natural disbelief that they can perform better.
- Creates an external business view.
- Raises the organization's level of maximum potential performance.[6]

The Importance of Benchmarks

As researched and reported by Christopher Bogan and Michael English in their publication, *Benchmarking for Best Practices,* "Historically, four important shifts in perspective have helped to elevate the importance of benchmarks in this performance measurement revolution:

1. Organizations now more than ever realize the importance of performance measurement or benchmarks in managing complex systems and processes.
2. Organizations now recognize customer satisfaction as a top priority.
3. Non-financial benchmarks are being developed and are providing management with important information necessary to achieve total quality excellence.
4. Information technology places powerful computer hardware and software within the reach of virtually every organization."[7]

Benchmarking is a methodical process involving some time-consuming techniques. While the steps do require the use of company resources, the ultimate benefits far outweigh the costs. Benchmarking techniques have generally proven to be a sound investment in time, especially considering that the knowledge obtained has been time-tested by others. Therefore, organi-

---

[6]Bogan, Christopher E., and Michael J. English, *Benchmarking for Best Practices* (New York, NY: McGraw-Hill, Inc., 1994), p. 14.
[7]Ibid, pp. 44-45.

zations performing benchmark techniques will reap the benefits to implementing quality processes which have already been proven.

Guidelines of Benchmark Development

When developing benchmarks, Bogan and English suggest four measurement elements which should serve as overall guidelines:

- Measurement focus.
- Measurement criteria.
- Measurement control.
- Ability to collect data.

Measurement Focus

- Determining where value for the customer is created in a work area or process.
- Determining where value is detracted through high costs, errors, rework, or accidents.
- Targeting benchmarks in areas where performance diverges from designated standards or where variation above and below standards is great.

Measurement Perspective

- Proactive - preventive elements called *leading indicators* because they foreshadow or predict future operational outcomes.
- Reactive - elements called *lagging indicators* because they describe the actual results of a system or process in a given time period.

Measurement Control

- Only those elements which can be controlled by the manager overseeing the process should be considered.

Data Collection

- Data should be collected from the benchmarks without incurring excessive collection costs.[8]

[8]Ibid, pp. 46-48.

There are 12 basic steps to effective development of benchmarks, which are outlined in Exhibit 5.1.

Exhibit 5.1
12 Steps to Effective Benchmarking

The following 12 steps illustrate a practical, systematic approach to successful benchmarking:

1. Identify your subject.
2. Identify test groups.
3. Collect and document the data.
4. Analyze the data.
5. Develop a benchmark.

   Based on the results of your study, the superior performers will now become the benchmark for your business process.

6. Communicate results.
7. Implement your findings.
8. Evaluate progress.
9. Develop improvement plan.
10. Review progress.
11. Standardize procedures.
12. Report results.

The project team is responsible for identifying the best possible solution given whatever limitations have been imposed by the team sponsor. Collaboration between the internal auditor and the other team members will occur when all facts have been gathered and the team begins their decision-making process.

After the team's recommendations have been accepted and implemented by the team sponsor, an implementation team may assume future responsibility. However, the original project team may be requested to support the implementation team's efforts by consulting with them on developing tracking mechanisms, developing process, time, and quality standards, and charting statistical controls. The internal auditor's responsibility to the project team will continue as long as the team remains intact.

Exhibit 5.2 illustrates two different project teams working on distinctly different issues. Both teams were formed in response to requests for assistance from organization management. Their missions, team structures, approaches, and reporting techniques are unique but tailored to fit their sponsor's purpose and needs.

Exhibit 5.2
A Study of Project Teams

The following scenarios will provide examples of several project teams, including their goals and objectives, team members, and assignments.

Example A: Depreciation of Company Assets

The chief financial officer of Company XYZ decided to form a team which will be responsible for evaluating whether the present method of depreciating company assets is the most financially beneficial to the company. The financial impacts of all methods under consideration would be identified and carefully analyzed. The CFO selected the following individuals to participate on the project team:

External Reporting Manager
Corporate Controller
Fixed Assets Manager
Tax Manager
Senior Internal Auditor
External Auditor Manager

The CFO designated the external reporting manager (ERM) to be the team leader for this project. The ERM is responsible for overseeing preparation of the company's annual report, resolving any reporting or accounting issues, and researching compliance issues. Therefore, the outcome of this project will have a direct impact on the responsibilities of the ERM, who will prepare any necessary footnotes for the annual report to account for changes in accounting treatment or methodology.

Exhibit 5.2 (Cont.)

The CFO and external reporting manager determined that this project should be completed in approximately three months, taking into consideration the deadline for financial statement preparation in accordance with their fiscal year end. At the kick-off meeting, a list of tasks was made which included the following:

- Compare company depreciation policies with industry benchmarks.
- Analyze the effect on product cost to change the depreciation methodology.
- Assess the accounting and business issues of changing the current methodology.
- Develop a comprehensive understanding of the useful lives of the products.

The internal auditor participated on the performance of each task, but was primarily responsible for benchmarking the depreciation methods used by other companies in the same industry and companies similar in asset size and activity level.

Once the project was complete, the team members met to discuss the results of their review and to develop their recommendations. A package summarizing their findings was prepared and presented to the sponsor. This package included documentation and charts of the findings which supported their conclusions. In addition, the package included what steps should be taken in preparing an implementation plan. Using the recommended method of depreciation, this plan identified all controls necessary for implementation and specific guidelines for usage.

Example B: An Accounting System Overhaul

The chief financial officer of a large company has determined, with the help of his managers, that the company is in need of an entirely new accounting system. The current system has been in place since the 1950s, and subsequent upgrades and modifications have not satisfactorily kept up with constant processing demands. As a result, the

Exhibit 5.2 (Cont.)

company managers have decided to implement a state-of-the-art system by the year 2000. Until then, an extensive amount of research, designing, and testing is necessary to ensure that the new accounting system will be able to meet the company's projected demands, perform in accordance with company, customer, and legal requirements, and have the capability of upgrading as necessary.

A project team has been formed with representatives from all appropriate disciplines to ensure that the new system is adequately developed and tested. The team consists of managers from Finance, Information Systems, and Accounting, supervisors and staff from Accounts Receivable, General Ledger Processing, Accounts Payable, Cost Allocations, and Internal Auditing, representatives from the external accounting firm, and several knowledgeable users. There are approximately 50 team members in all. For this extensive effort, the CFO, acting as sponsor, has designated the manager of finance to be the team leader, and he, in turn, has assigned lead positions to the managers of information systems and accounting. The purpose of this project is to:

- Develop software which will be capable of performing the accounting transactions necessary for the company.
- Produce the needed business reports and financial data.
- Establish appropriate internal controls to ensure integrity of accounting data.

The project team has been broken down into subgroups for each participating discipline. A weekly meeting is held for all team members. At this meeting, weekly accomplishments are reported and goals are reviewed. A weekly "issues" meeting is also held by leaders of subgroups to discuss project deadlines, budget considerations, and critical issues.

The project will be completed in several distinct segments:

- Start-up (write charter/make assignments).
- Design and analysis (conceptual phase of design).

Exhibit 5.2 (Cont.)

- Global configuration (high-level design).
- Configuration (in-depth design).
- Business day simulation (testing system using test data).
- Implementation (procedures and controls executed).

Internal auditing's role in this project will be critical during the design and analysis phase. The auditors have been asked to review the design for the test data, which will be assigned a known output. In addition, the auditors will review the controls planned for the various accounting transactions and make recommendations to enhance the controls or to add or delete controls as necessary. Internal auditing plans to issue interim memos to the sponsor at the conclusion of each project phase. Internal auditing will also report their final conclusions and recommendations in an internal memo to the sponsor and the key managers at the conclusion of their involvement.

Chapter Summary

Although the team concept is relatively new to American business, its value and benefits are already being recognized by modern, dynamic organizations. These organizations employ project teams to assist in identifying solutions to tough business problems, analyze work processes to become more economically sound and streamlined, and in performing highly sensitive investigations. The unique procedures employed by project teams enable them to devise feasible solutions to difficult circumstances. The team's greatest asset is in the diversity of business minds which come together for a common purpose.

As a marketing tool, audit participation on project teams has been beneficial overall in winning management's praise and support. Internal auditing brings a unique perspective to project teams through their background and training. Reluctance to include internal audit is usually the result of individuals with the organization fearing an unwanted audit or that the auditors will take an unduly negative position on specific proposals.

With a carefully orchestrated marketing approach, internal auditors can promote themselves as the experts they are and market their abilities and unique talents to organization management. As project teams begin to establish a successful track record, internal auditing will likely be asked to participate in a greater number of future partnership opportunities.

CHAPTER 6 MEASURING AND IMPROVING PERFORMANCE

While measuring our performance is important, it is much more important that we discover how the customer measures our performance. The ultimate value of our organization is measured in terms of customer satisfaction.

— Lockheed Corporation
Guidelines and Tools for Continuous Improvement

Monitoring Effectiveness Through Feedback

An important aspect of any marketing program includes obtaining feedback from audit customers. Ongoing feedback from the marketplace is an absolute requirement. Essential to measuring the marketing techniques of every audit department is understanding how the *customer* measures their performance. For an audit department to fully understand their marketing effectiveness and to be able to make suitable changes to their marketing approach, style, or methodology depends largely on how well their services are received and appreciated by their customers.

Understanding the audit customers' expectations is the first step in developing a viable performance measurement system. According to John Zenger, founder of Zenger-Miller, Inc., an internationally known training and consulting firm, the perceptions of all potential customers should be considered.

We can apply this concept to internal auditors just as other service providers would consider the perceptions of their own customers. Internal auditors should not only know who their audit customers are, but should interview each to gain an understanding of their individual expectations. Awareness of these expectations may be important in shaping the marketing plan's focus and objectives. *Once auditors know their customers' needs and requirements, they will be able to develop ways to measure themselves and their performance.*

Knowing your customers' key expectations helps to avoid wasting time marketing services the customers do not care about or, worse, modifications to those services which leave customers less satisfied than before. The better internal auditors understand these expectations, the better able they will be to adjust the marketing plan to meet them. If possible, auditors should ask their customers for specific expectations in order to measure the success of subsequent improvement efforts. Although expectations will vary depending on the product or service, the following are common categories of customer expectations and a related question for each:

Category	**Related Questions**
Timeliness	Were audit services provided in a timely manner?
Reliability	Were the observations and suggestions reliable?
Accuracy	Were the observations factual and accurate?
Ease of use	Were the auditors considerate in their use of your time?
Extra service	What other services could we provide to you?[1]

Internal auditors need feedback from their audit customers in order to gauge the effectiveness of their marketing efforts. They may receive an occasional written or verbal commendation from an audit customer as a result of outstanding performance of a review. However, without a system of monitoring overall customer satisfaction, auditors may be unaware of any dissatisfaction. Even one dissatisfied customer can negatively influence the internal auditor's reputation through informal communication with other organization managers.

Any external feedback from audit customers is considered an indicator of performance. Performance indicators are events which lead to preliminary conclusions about whether goals and objectives will be met. They are the outcome of comparing actual with desired results in order to provide feedback relating to the performance of an organization.

Performance indicators are useful tools in shaping management's opinion of their organization's performance. When applied in a systematic way, managers can identify areas where their marketing efforts were unsatisfactory and take the necessary action. Performance indicators identify poor versus outstanding performers and indicate improvements in specific pro-

[1]Zenger, John H., Ed Musselwhite, Kathleen Hurson, and Craig Perrin, *Leading Teams: Mastering the New Role* (Illinois/New York: Irwin Professional Publishing, 1994), pp. 148-149.

cesses and operations. Customer feedback is the most reliable indicator of audit performance as a result of marketing efforts.

The ultimate value of the internal auditing department is measured in terms of customer satisfaction. To understand and gauge the level of satisfaction resulting from marketing techniques employed by internal auditing, auditors may stimulate their audit customers to rate their performance by employing the following direct methods:

- ***Written evaluations.*** The audit manager can request responsible organization managers to provide a written evaluation of internal auditing's marketing techniques. This evaluation should include their candid response to these techniques and whether their perception of internal audit changed at the conclusion of whatever service was provided (i.e., regular audit, management-requested consulting review, project team participation, etc.). Alternatively, the audit manager may request the responsible company manager to complete an "Audit Effectiveness Questionnaire" regarding the manner in which the audit was conducted in addition to questions regarding marketing aspects. These evaluations should enable the audit manager to obtain a good understanding of marketing strengths and weaknesses. A standard questionnaire is presented in Exhibit 6.1.

- ***Direct contact.*** The audit supervisor or director may choose to contact organization management personally and candidly ask for their perception of internal auditing's marketing program. Depending on the type of response, the audit manager may decide to employ personal marketing techniques while soliciting new concerns from the audit customer. These concerns can be translated into future audit reviews through this method of personal interaction with the audit customer.

- ***Audit customer surveys.*** Annual or periodic surveys may be conducted by the audit manager by personally contacting or meeting with each department head and members of executive management. These surveys are a positive way to solicit candid information from the organization's management regarding internal auditing's marketing program, their perception or image of internal auditing, current or potential operational concerns, and any suggestions for improvement in audit services. These surveys are instrumental in pointing out deficiencies in internal auditing's marketing strategy. In addition, conducting surveys is another effective method of marketing internal auditing's services, and it can be helpful in predicting scheduling requirements for future audits or management-requested reviews.

Exhibit 6.1
Audit Effectiveness Questionnaire

To help us in our efforts to provide value-added audit services to the company, please provide responses regarding your recent involvement with the internal auditing department. For each item below, please circle the number that best reflects your answer to the corresponding question. We would be interested in any additional comments you might have.

1. Describe the nature of your most recent involvement with internal auditing.

2. Did this involvement occur as a result of solicitation or other marketing communication by internal auditing? If so, describe the method of communication (i.e., phone contact, personal meeting, letter, etc.).

3. Did this communication prompt you to request internal auditing to perform a specific review or other consulting service?

4. What audit service was provided to you?

	Extremely			Not at All	
5. How knowledgeable do you rate yourself regarding the services currently provided by internal auditing?	5	4	3	2	1

	Yes			Not at All	
6. Did the audit service provided to you add value to your operation?	5	4	3	2	1

	Yes			Not at All	
7. Are you now better able to effectively discharge your responsibilities?	5	4	3	2	1

Exhibit 6.1 (Cont.)

	Very Clearly				Not at All
8. Was the purpose of the review/service clearly established and agreed upon?	5	4	3	2	1
	Very Consistent				**Not at All**
9. Was the stated purpose consistent with your operations and concerns?	5	4	3	2	1
	Excellent				**Poor**
10. How do you rate the quality of the findings and recommendations?	5	4	3	2	1
	Very Satisfied				**Not at All**
11. Overall, how would you rate your satisfaction with the service provided?	5	4	3	2	1

12. What changes do you suggest to improve internal auditing's communication with company management and their overall marketing process?

13. What changes do you suggest to make internal auditing's services more value added?

14. Based on your experience, will you request assistance from internal auditing in the future?

Please provide any other comments about this review which you feel will:

- Help us to evaluate the quality or effectiveness of our marketing process.
- Help to improve our audit process.

Developing a Performance Measurement System

In order to draw logical conclusions based on factual data, internal auditors must obtain precise data about the quality of audit services which resulted directly or indirectly from their marketing program. This data can then be compared with their audit customers' key expectations. After making a comparison of key expectations to actual performance, the auditors will know what areas require improvements that will more closely align the output of a given work process with customers' key expectations. The next step is to determine whether the discrepancies can be corrected or otherwise modified to more closely conform to their customers' expectations. Using analytical skills, the auditors can later identify all available options for improving the work process or activity.

Assessing the original marketing program requires a strict review of each marketing component to determine whether results:

- Were substantially achieved.
- Were partially achieved.
- Could not be determined.
- Were unsatisfactory.

In order to gauge whether internal auditing is achieving their goals and objectives for specific marketing activities, the audit manager must apply specific criteria to be able to measure the organization's performance. Once actual performance has been compared to established goals and objectives, discrepancies can be identified for management's review and resolution.

This process is called a ***performance measurement system***. Such a system will enable audit management to measure the success of their marketing efforts, determine areas of weakness, and redirect their efforts for successful continuation. Establishing performance standards and measuring the achievement of goals and objectives are two critical components of managing any activity. Without an effective way to measure the performance of each activity, managers cannot identify potential problems and gauge operational improvements.

Maintaining an aggressive marketing program is the result of internal auditing's ability to identify its flawed or ineffective components. Internal auditing, like any organization, is only as effective as its processes, or activities. Activities are consumers of resources and should be assessed not only in terms of the value they add, but also in terms of the amount of capital, people, time, equipment, and material they require to produce that value.

While each activity exists to make a contribution to one or more organizational goals, its effectiveness is a major variable in the achievement of those goals. Therefore, each activity should be measured against criteria that reflects the contribution that the activity is expected to make toward internal auditing's marketing goals.

To avoid confusion, the specific activity being measured must be precisely defined. These measurements should reflect internal auditing's performance in terms of the following:

- **Effectiveness:** actual output compared with expected output.
- **Efficiency:** resources planned with respect to resources actually used.
- **Quality:** degree of customer satisfaction.
- **Productivity:** output compared with input.
- **Quality of work life:** degree of job satisfaction.
- **Innovation:** creative process that responds to change.[2]

The purpose of developing and establishing a performance measurement system is to obtain objective or quantitative data to determine the effectiveness of the activity being measured. This data is necessary to determine whether improvements in the activity are required. Establishing a sound measurement system will ensure the right things are being monitored, rather than a collection of unrelated, and potentially counterproductive, measures. Moreover, the measurement system must be able to convert the data provided into intelligent action.

Effective measurement systems must:

- Relate directly to what constitutes performance.
- Be simple yet effective.
- Measure processes, activities, and organizations, not individuals.
- Be accepted by owners of the activity.
- Be designed to lead to improvement.

---

[2]*Guidelines and Tools for Continuous Improvement,* Lockheed Corporation, 1994, p. 54.

- Measure items that can be controlled by the group.
- Enable customer feedback.
- Measure only the importance parameters.
- Measure characteristics related to customer requirements and expectations.
- Be stated in objective, quantifiable terms in order to enable accurate measurement.
- Relate to time, cost, efficiency, accuracy, or other critical quality-related aspects of a process or activity.[3]

The development of a performance measurement system to support organizational analysis or process management is a structured process that ensures that essential criteria and characteristics of a good measurement system are addressed. Lockheed Corporation, a prime defense contractor, examined this process in their 1994 internal publication, *Guidelines and Tools for Continuous Improvement*, which is illustrated and discussed in Exhibit 6.2.

Exhibit 6.2
Developing a Performance Measurement System[4]

Step 1 — Identify the Performing Group. The performing group is made up of employees involved in the improvement process. They could belong to a single organization or be discrete members of cross-functional organizations working as a team to improve a process. Members must agree on the group's mission, customers, and basic process before they develop performance indicators.

Step 2 — Meet with Customers to Explain Methods. As points or elements of the process being monitored are identified, internal and external customers must be involved. Identification of monitor points will greatly aid in future problem-solving activity. The group leader must ensure that customer inputs are incorporated in the measurement process.

---

[3]Ibid.

[4]Ibid, pp. 56-57.

Exhibit 6.2 (Cont.)

Step 3 — Define the Measurements (Cost, Quality, Schedule, etc.). Identifying key performance characteristics is as important as developing the tools that measure them. Indicators for both good and bad performance must be developed, and the data source for each indicator must be identified and defined.

Step 4 — Gather Data and Report. Data must be given to the team members for problem solving. If the data is sent outside the group, it should be provided as an informational database for other teams or groups. Feedback is not a one-time event but rather the essence of the continuous improvement process.

Step 5 — Establish Review Cycle. Management decides who will receive and review data reports and how feedback will be given to the team. The purpose of feedback is to improve the measurement system. The group leader has overall responsibility for improving the measurement system.

Performance Measurement System (adapted with permission from Lockheed Corporation, 1994)

The following table provides broad criteria for performance measurement along with customer expectations to provide an example of how audit services can be measured in terms of their effectiveness. We will assume that our customer in this case is organization management.

Activity	Customer Expectations	Actual Performance	Action Needed
Type of review: consultative reviews, participation on project teams, efficiency or cost savings reviews, reviews of control environments, etc.	Expectations should include specific performance (quality, efficiency, productivity, effectiveness, innovation) for a set period of time.	Audit performance measured in customer terms that actually occurred during that time period.	Discrepancies constitute unmet expectations. Marketing actions should be developed to address these issues.

Developing a Continuous Improvement Plan

The primary purpose of a performance measurement system is to support the continuous improvement process. As continuous improvement becomes part of everyday activities, organizations benefit from increases in competitiveness, profitability, financial strength, flexibility, and growth. As the organization benefits, so does every employee. As the system yields results, the continuous improvement attitude builds.[5]

Perhaps the most important aspect of continuous improvement is its systematic approach. This approach requires careful study and planning before change is made to ensure the right process is changed and that the change is beneficial to the operation.

When undertaking the development of a continuous improvement plan, a concise, yet comprehensive, methodology for managing this process can be used. Before this methodology can be effectively applied, however, a vision of continuous improvement must be instilled in the performing organization.

Although the continuous improvement process can be initiated by individuals or members of management, utilizing project teams with appointed members has proven to be a superior method of developing meaningful process improvements. For project teams to be effective, they must be empowered by management to study the process, identify improvements, and take action.[6]

There are 12 basic steps to implementing continuous improvement, as follows:

1. ***Identify processes and their associated criticality.*** In order to employ the organization's resources in the most beneficial manner, all processes of interest should be identified and prioritized with respect to criticality of the product/service and the customer.

2. ***Select process for improvement and define ownership.*** When selecting the process for review, one of the best ways of evaluating the process candidates is from a cost standpoint. Those processes that

[5]*Guidelines and Tools for Continuous Improvement*, Lockheed Corporation, 1994, pp. 6-7.
[6]Ibid, p. 13.

have the greatest potential to provide value or those with significant potential for company loss are selected for improvement first. Typical processes for improvement are characterized by:

- Poor cost performance.
- Low capability.
- Problem history.
- Criticality to customer satisfaction and acceptance.
- Effect on product life, reliability, and performance.

A clear process owner and boundary definition must be identified for each selected process. Boundary definition includes location, number of employees involved within the process, products affected, and customers.

3. ***Define customer requirements.*** Identification of the customer, or user of the product or service, is important. Without knowledge of customer requirements, it is impossible to understand the necessity for or the significance of a process. To improve a process, we must know how our customer intends to use the process outcome, which will also enable us to understand which process improvements will increase product usability.

4. ***Organize an improvement team.*** The next step is to develop a project team to work on the improvement project. Among the advantages of using teams is the expanded skill base for addressing the improvement issues and the ability to segment tasks and accomplish them in parallel.

   Coordination is required to get people with the greatest chance of success assigned to the team. Team effectiveness depends on management involvement, either in direct contact or working as part of the team, and communication of team findings. Implementation of the proposals made by the team must be supported by management.

5. ***Develop an improvement plan.*** The development of a formal process improvement plan is key to keeping the project on schedule. Such a plan should include:

   - A diagram showing the tasks and their interrelationships over time.
   - Estimated completion dates.

- Personnel and cost estimates.
- Change coordination.
- Measures of effectiveness.

Although recommendations for actual process improvements may not be developed at this stage, having a plan enables the team to coordinate the improvement activities and time sequences.

6. ***Review the current process.*** Process review is a systematic and comprehensive evaluation of the operation of a process. A process review is a structured assessment of the current condition of a process. Without a thorough understanding of the current process, effective recommendations for improvements cannot be made. A comprehensive process review may be performed using these suggested steps:

   - Development of a detailed flowchart of the process.
   - Review of documented procedures including control points.
   - Observation of personnel performing process tasks to establish what is actually done (undocumented procedures).
   - Review of performance indicators (customer feedback, etc.).
   - Validation of process performance measurements.
   - Review of boundaries and interfaces (other organizations, customers, etc.).
   - Baseline current process or product performance.
   - Review of documented accept/reject criteria.

   Once the process review is complete, the team summarizes its findings and makes recommendations, with the assistance of the process owner.

7. ***Establish measures of performance.*** The process owner should be able to define the important quality characteristics of the process. To effectively establish a measure of performance, the following must be addressed:

   - Requirements: What must we have from the process?
   - Capability: What level of performance is possible?
   - Conformance: What has the process performance been?
   - Improvement: What can we do to make the process better?
   - Risk: What problems may we encounter with this process?

8. ***Analyze process and identify improvements.*** Although we may frequently understand the process requirements, we may have no idea what causes the problems in the processes involved. Problem-solving methodologies may be utilized at this point in the process improvement strategy.

9. ***Implement the process change.*** Improvement must be effectively managed in order to minimize disruption and resistance. Company change practices should be reviewed to ensure consistency with improvement recommendation and conformance to company change practices. Process improvement should be implemented only once process interrelationships and task functions are understood. Processes should be restructured, streamlined, shortened, or otherwise changed to agree with critical success factors established by the customer. Changes should be properly communicated to all affected employees, documented, and coordinated with customers.

10. ***Validate process improvement effectiveness.*** Improvement may be validated through established performance measurements. Significant improvements can be verified against baseline performance measurements identified prior to implementation of process improvement. Process improvement has occurred if customer satisfaction has increased, costs are reduced, reliability has improved, or variability has been reduced.

11. ***Establish and maintain controls.*** Process controls are required to ensure that quality improvements do not lose their effectiveness over time. Several control strategies are key:

    - Designing a process so that the likelihood of error is low (e.g., converting a manual data entry system to a bar-code data entry system).

    - Timely feedback to the employees or systems associated with the process, including frequent communication, real-time information availability, identification of process monitoring features, and integration of feedback into standard operating methods.

12. ***Continuously improve.*** Once the project is complete, the team should be disbanded, and other projects with different team members may be formed for additional improvement strategies. The improvement

process should continue with individuals who continually seek opportunities for improvement, thereby increasing customer satisfaction and the utility of the end product.[7]

Good processes make good products and services. Continuous improvement techniques are only as effective as the commitment to excellence displayed by the project team, sponsor, and responsible management. Continuous improvement techniques have been proven effective by those audit organizations willing to invest the critical time and resources necessary to make improvements a reality. The continuous improvement methodology focuses on improving the work processes that result in deliverable products and services. The continuous improvement goal is to eliminate activities that add no value and bottlenecks that stand in the way of superior performance.[8]

Why Performance Measurement Systems Fail

While the benefits and merits of performance measurement systems have been described at length, the potential failure of these systems is still a very real possibility and can occur for one of several reasons. For example, if the process measurements are imposed by audit management but are not accepted by the performing group (internal auditing staff), the resulting data may be completely unreliable and misrepresented. For this reason, it is important to include the performing group in the development process.

Another reason for failure is if fear evolves from the exposure of either good or bad performance. The performing group may be satisfied with maintaining a status quo on their performance. If management fails to ultimately reward outstanding performance or performance improvements, the performing group will view this as a demotivator. Improper definition of the system or process to be measured or failure to consider customer requirements will also result in subsequent failure. Last, but not least, failure may result from too much time spent in gathering data and reporting instead of on analysis and action.[9]

---

[7]Ibid, pp. 38-43.
[8]Ibid, p. 5.
[9]Ibid, p. 57.

Peter F. Drucker coined the term "management by objective" (MBO), which is the concept of integrating the individual's objectives with those of the company.[10] Sawyer takes this concept one step further by challenging internal auditors to compare MBO accomplishments against goals. Internal auditing may identify failure in their own performance measurement system by using the following indicators as evidence of the breakdown:

- Management may set requirements, then forget about them.
- Objectives are not properly explained to subordinates.
- Guidelines and premises were not specified and, therefore, goals are not reasonable.
- Management sets forth procedures, not goals.
- Company objectives are at fault because they are inconsistent, unrealistic, or unclear.
- Goals are not quantified and so accomplishments are not measured.
- Goals are either continually being changed or are completely inflexible.
- Managers are not equipped with accurate, current information to help themselves.[11]

While failure can occur, performance measurement systems which are developed in accordance with the steps previously mentioned will be less likely to fail. It is audit management's responsibility to ensure that performance standards are properly communicated to and supported by the individuals who are responsible for performing the tasks. A system that accurately measures performance can increase the productivity of the audit organization and the satisfaction of internal auditors when applied in accordance with known and accepted criteria.

Chapter Summary

Strategies for improving the weakest components of the marketing program must be developed to meet future challenges. In order for internal auditing to gauge the effectiveness of their marketing efforts, a system of performance measurement is essential. A measurement system which en-

---

[10]Drucker, Peter F., *Management: Tasks, Responsibilities, Practices* (New York, NY: Harper & Row Publishers, Inc., 1974), pp. 430-440.
[11]Sawyer, Lawrence B., and Mortimer A. Dittenhofer, *Sawyer's Internal Auditing: The Practice of Modern Internal Auditing* (Altamonte Springs, FL.: The Institute of Internal Auditors, 1996), pp. 1148-1149.

ables internal auditing to identify trouble areas and measure improvement over time will be key to ensuring its longevity and success.

Because perceptions are difficult to measure, a continual feedback system between internal auditors and their customers is necessary. It is important for internal auditors to continually assess their marketing efforts in order to evaluate their performance in terms of attitude, service, diligence, and timeliness. Whether customer surveys, questionnaires, or the direct contact approach is used to collect feedback, all audit customer comments must be considered in the quest to provide outstanding services.

CONCLUSION THE NEXT STEP

The best way to destroy the enemy is to make him...one's friend. Where the proposed friend is an internal auditor, that will take a good deal of marketing; but in the long range it is worth it.

— Lawrence B. Sawyer
Sawyer's Internal Auditing:
The Practice of Modern Internal Auditing

Meeting New Demands

The role of internal auditing first emerged when organization management realized an unsatisfied need — *to thoroughly monitor organization operations at all levels.* Internal auditing was thus created to be an independent assessor of company operations. Now, in the 1990s, management is recognizing yet another unsatisfied need, one that challenges internal auditors to extend their traditional parameters and flex their creative muscles. This need requires internal auditing to understand and share management's business philosophy in order to better contribute to organization goals and objectives.

For obvious reasons, auditors should be concerned with providing value which will more than offset their expense to their organization. Maintaining a full-time audit department directly affects an organization's profit margin. Because management scrutinizes the "bottom line," they also question the singular value of individual organization expenses and overhead. Internal auditors are receiving the same kind of scrutiny and must demonstrate how their continued services justify their position.

Exploring ways to stay flexible to meet the needs of organization managers will ensure that internal auditing remains a valuable organizational asset. The best way to accomplish this task is to pursue the benefits that a marketing strategy has to offer. This concept of marketing may be relatively new to internal auditors. In the past, they found security in the knowledge that their recommendations would be readily accepted and implemented by management. However, times have changed. Recommendations are now scrutinized for intrinsic value and future payoffs before they are accepted. Internal auditors no longer have the security that enveloped them in the 1980s. In the 1990s and beyond, they will be asked to provide tangible evidence that they can make viable contributions to the welfare of the organization. Here is where the value of a comprehensive, well-defined marketing program will be recognized and appreciated.

Internal auditing has, until now, been an underutilized organization resource with vast potential to be tapped. As a result, management is only now becoming aware of the potential benefits of employing audit resources. To effectively market their abilities and skills will require internal auditors to court organization executives and develop stable working relationships with operating managers.

The success of a marketing program depends on the auditor's ability to seek and create *marketing opportunities* for the purpose of making economic contributions to their organization. Some may argue that the best marketing strategy is to simply provide an excellent quality of service, thereby creating value for their customers. In theory, this approach sounds good, but its implementation is too vague and undisciplined. Instead, internal auditors must rely on a well-defined set of goals and objectives as a basis for promoting and marketing their services.

From Concept to Success

Once audit managers realize that marketing their department is an inevitable task and a necessity for successful continuation, they will embark on a rigorous, but potentially profitable, journey. Marketing to build and improve public relations is key to the internal auditor's success.

Most marketing efforts are achieved through one-on-one interaction with auditees. Marketing must be learned and continually practiced and perfected. It is an ongoing process, the positive and negative impacts of which must be clearly understood by the internal auditing staff and management. Negative marketing, which can occur at any time given a wrong impression or misinterpretation, can be difficult to overcome. The impacts brought about by negative perceptions from auditees can be extremely detrimental to the internal auditor's reputation and standing.

Marketing in the true sense of the word, then, is an unending process. It is safe to say that the next step in the marketing process is to start over and reassess the original marketing plan for ways to improve upon it, align its concepts with organization goals and objectives, ensure that audit duties are performed while providing quality consulting services to management, and streamline it to make it more economically sound and effective. To avoid getting lost in business rhetoric, here are some practical suggestions for continuing and enhancing an established marketing strategy:

- ***Develop a learning organization.*** Often, maintaining an excellent reputation is closely linked with improving and encouraging organizational learning. The learning organization encourages collaborative learning, thinking, and doing. Individual improvements and achievements lead to team, process, and organizational excellence.

  An audit director who is concerned with the quality of his audit services should encourage his staff and managers to participate in appropriate training classes and seminars, both internal and external to the organization, and in management-sponsored project teams when possible. Individual or team partnering with other organization personnel can provide an excellent opportunity to increase the knowledge of the participating auditor, who can then pass on the gained insight to the department.

  In addition, the internal auditing staff and management should improve their marketing research techniques by remaining watchful of industry issues, events, and government legislation which could impact future operations. Internal auditing has a leadership responsibility to inform their organization management of such events.

- ***Establish criteria for improvement.*** Assuming that a marketing plan has been established and put into action for a period of time, audit management should now reassess its strengths and weaknesses. Systematically reviewing every aspect of the plan is necessary to understand how it can be made better for both the audit department and the organization.

  For example, the audit manager should analyze the number of hours budgeted for management-requested reviews. This amount should be compared with actual usage and further analyzed for marketing effectiveness and for adequacy in meeting company managers' demands. If the demand was low, resulting in a partially unused budget, then the audit manager should examine the methods he used to communicate and market his intended use of this budget to management. If the budgeted amount was exceeded, then the audit manager may assume that the marketing plan succeeded, and may decide to allocate a larger hourly budget for the upcoming year.

Some internal auditing departments have used a zero-based budgeting technique to determine how many hours to allocate to management requests. This technique requires the audit manager to interview every key department head in the organization and solicit upcoming or current concerns. These concerns can then be anticipated for future reviews and scheduled accordingly. While this method is time-consuming, it is an excellent method for marketing internal auditing to organization management on an individual basis.

Aside from the actual budgeting process, some other components of the marketing plan that should be reassessed for effectiveness include:

- Customer base (i.e., identification, logistics).
- Interaction with customers (i.e., frequency, levels of management, situational activities).
- Methods of advertising and communicating plan (i.e., channels, frequency of communication).
- Marketing research and resources (i.e., industry/organization events, external influences).

Understanding where the weaknesses exist is the first step to establishing new and improved criteria for an ongoing marketing plan. Revised criteria translates into a new set of goals and objectives for audit management to achieve.

- ***Solicit feedback from company personnel.*** An important tool for uncovering weaknesses or problems with a marketing plan may be in directly contacting various organization managers and requesting information or other feedback on their overall perception of internal auditing.

  A basic questionnaire (similar to the one in Chapter 6) could be developed to standardize this process. The main objective is to get an impression of management's acceptance of internal auditing's services, their perception of the competence and professionalism of the audit staff, and their awareness of internal auditing's marketing techniques. In order to promote candid responses, the audit manager may encourage organization managers to submit their responses anonymously. Otherwise, managers may worry about potential repercussions if an adverse or uncomplimentary response is submitted.

- ***Market and promote internal auditing as a service provider.*** Internal auditing is a service organization, providing specialized, technical services to their organization. When judging the professional quality of a service occupation, specific criteria may be used. The nature of service providers requires internal auditors to consider this criteria when marketing themselves to management. An effective marketing plan should include the following criteria which designates internal auditing as a professional service provider:

    - The spectrum of services provided to management.
    - Specialized training and personal achievements.
    - Credentials (including licensure or certifications).
    - Professionalism (including memberships in related associations).
    - Code of ethics and business philosophies.
    - Continuing educational requirements.

- ***Benchmark critical processes.*** Sometimes the best method of improving a product is to determine where it stands in relation to other industry performers. This process, called benchmarking, strives to identify the outstanding leaders and to pattern performance based on their accomplishments. The same philosophy holds true for internal audit.

    The majority of the information in this publication was predicated on the systems and techniques currently practiced by modern-day audit entrepreneurs. Any audit manager can use benchmarking techniques to identify new and creative ways to improve his marketing plan. The simplest approach is to contact other audit managers and inquire as to their specific marketing procedures, how long they have been established, and what the results have garnered. Based on the responses obtained, an audit manager should be able to pick and choose those procedures and techniques which are best suited for his department.

Benchmarking does not tolerate benchwarmers. The most important aspect of benchmarking is that it keeps audit managers constantly thinking in terms of improving their marketing process. Dynamic performance and innovative techniques will be the key to successful marketing. Proven processes will be quickly embraced by audit managers seeking to advance their department's visibility, reputation, and status within the organization.

- ***Consider a name change.*** As internal auditors enlarge their responsibilities to include those of internal consultants, many are also modifying their personal or departmental business titles to reflect this change. The title "internal auditor" invokes images of a police officer, critic, faultfinder, or judge. Therefore, if an internal auditor wants to promote himself as management's partner, he may opt to modify his title accordingly. For example, some modern, unique business titles currently used include:

  - Internal consultant.
  - Integrated consulting and auditing.
  - Business process analyst.
  - Business systems analyst.
  - Information systems analyst.

Partnering with Management: The Final Solution

Organization management is concerned with maintaining a competitive edge against ever-increasing customer demands for higher quality, lower prices, and more expeditious service. If management's top priority is customer satisfaction and cost savings, then improving and streamlining operations is necessary to accomplish their goals. Internal auditors now have a prime opportunity to expand their traditional auditing roles by offering their services to organization management.

A dynamic marketing plan is the ideal vehicle for mapping a plan of action for advancing the auditing department. A well-devised plan will launch the auditors as internal consultants. As internal auditors build a respected reputation as internal consultants, they will be in demand and invited to collaborate with organization managers in resolving problems or by participating in other decision-making activities.

Gil Amelio, Chairman & CEO of Apple Computer, once said,

> "Selling a product is not a matter of using a 'bag of tricks.' It is the careful attention to the customer's business and the development of solutions to problems that impede his success. Furthermore, ... it includes the ability to partner with our customers to create new sources of revenue for them that will allow them to compete in their own arenas."

This statement can be applied to internal auditors who are interested in partnering with their organization management for the purpose of developing ways to economize and streamline operations. Whenever operational improvements can be found, a cost savings will be realized by the organization, which, in many cases, translates into greater revenue through a reduction of expenses. In this sense, both managers and internal auditors share a similar goal and vision for the organization. Collaborating with each other for the good of the organization becomes a natural part of their relationship.

Internal auditors serve a valuable role in the research and detection of imprudent systems and unnecessary processes. They are proficient at recommending suitable methodologies which can restore a measure of profitability and productivity to ailing operations. Internal auditors partnering with management are not bound by the chains of compliance auditing and are free to recommend ways to streamline and improve work processes.

Through automation of previously manual tasks, unnecessary tasks and task duplication become evident and correctable. Measurable cost savings allow an organization to realize an improvement in their profit margin, which may potentially result in operational expansion or other growth opportunities. Auditors who provide quantifiable data to management in conjunction with their recommendations for improvement will assert their continuing value to the organization and secure future opportunities for the same.

This study has discussed several ways that partnering with management can be performed, including audit activities which cover:

- Economy and efficiency issues.
- Automation of operations.
- Operational streamlining.

- Changes in control environments.
- Benchmarks of company performance.
- Participation on project teams.
- Investigations of covert issues.

The internal auditor's job is to sustain this collaborative process by continuing the marketing strategy with new and improved techniques that appeal to management. This process will hinge on the internal auditor's commitment to developing effective information gathering techniques, such as marketing research and customer development activities, as dictated by the marketing plan.

With consideration to the information and suggestions that have been provided in this study, the bottom line must be this: *marketing the internal auditing function is key to successful contribution in the 1990s and beyond.* A well-developed marketing program will enable audit management to chart a strategy, monitor their department's progress, and make appropriate changes.

Changes will be dictated by management's acceptance of internal auditing's services, the audit services offered, and the marketing techniques used to promote the auditing department. Management's perception of internal auditing's value to the organization must be constantly nurtured. After all, an internal auditing department that remains flexible by recognizing and acting upon the potential demands and future opportunities of auditing will be a continuing asset to their organization.